RIDING THE
BLUE TRAIN

RIDING THE BLUE TRAIN

A Leadership Plan for Explosive Growth

BART SAYLE and
SURINDER KUMAR

PORTFOLIO

PORTFOLIO
Published by the Penguin Group
Penguin Group (USA) Inc., 375 Hudson Street, New York, New York 10014, U.S.A.
Penguin Group (Canada), 90 Eglinton Avenue East, Suite 700, Toronto, Ontario,
Canada M4P 2Y3 (a division of Pearson Penguin Canada Inc.)
Penguin Books Ltd, 80 Strand, London WC2R 0RL, England
Penguin Ireland, 25 St. Stephen's Green, Dublin 2, Ireland (a division of Penguin Books Ltd)
Penguin Books Australia Ltd, 250 Camberwell Road, Camberwell, Victoria 3124, Australia
(a division of Pearson Australia Group Pty Ltd)
Penguin Books India Pvt Ltd, 11 Community Centre, Panchsheel Park,
New Delhi – 110 017, India
Penguin Group (NZ), Cnr Airborne and Rosedale Roads, Albany, Auckland 1310,
New Zealand (a division of Pearson New Zealand Ltd)
Penguin Books (South Africa) (Pty) Ltd, 24 Sturdee Avenue, Rosebank, Johannesburg 2196,
South Africa

Penguin Books Ltd, Registered Offices: 80 Strand, London WC2R 0RL, England

First published in 2006 by Portfolio, a member of Penguin Group (USA) Inc.

10 9 8 7 6 5 4 3 2 1

PUBLISHER'S NOTE:
This publication is designed to provide accurate and authoritative information in regard to
the subject matter covered. It is sold with the understanding that the publisher is not engaged
in rendering legal, accounting or other professional services. If you require legal advice or
other expert assistance, you should seek the services of a competent professional.

LIBRARY OF CONGRESS CATALOGING IN PUBLICATION DATA
Sayle, Bart.
  Riding the blue train : a leadership plan for explosive growth / Bart Sayle and Surinder
Kumar.
    p. cm.
  Includes index.
  Contents: The breakthrough journey—The power of magical thinking—The five powers—
Empowering and limiting beliefs—Red train, blue train—Breakthrough communications—
Full-on—Line of one—Breakthrough leader—Achieving the future.
  ISBN 1-59184-135-6
  1. Corporate culture.   2. Organizational behavior.   I. Kumar, Surinder.   II. Title.
  HD58.7.R53   2006
  658.3'01—dc22   2006048329

Printed in the United States of America

This book is dedicated to our readers who, as leaders, choose to develop great people and inspire them to Ride the Blue Train.

FOREWORD

Exceptional leaders seek out every opportunity to inspire growth, energy, and creativity among their people . . . and for the best leaders, this is a tireless pursuit.

It's a formidable challenge given the myriad factors at work today that stifle creative energy. Fear of failure, time and cost pressures, and comfort with the status quo all erode a company's ability to innovate.

What Does It Take to Stimulate Innovation in the Workplace?

For a company such as ours—one with a heritage that spanned generations of leaders and worldwide associates—change and revolutionary innovation could have been met with deep resistance. Yet, together, we found a way to respect the past while doing what was right for our future. In my experience, stimulating innovation requires both letting go of entrenched approaches and structures as well as embracing new growth aspirations and mind-sets.

Think about the creative energy of a child. Children have little fear of the unknown and are totally open to new experiences. For them, it's all about curiosity, experimentation, unbridled energy, and discovery.

How do we replicate that creative process . . . that intense desire to learn, problem solve, create, and grow . . . in our day-to-day work settings?

For the Wm. Wrigley Jr. Company, growth and innovation required building on the values that made our company unique, establishing a set of High Performance Principles to guide our behaviors and our operating approach, and—importantly—leveraging the talent and commitment of our people across the globe. By incorporating the principles of Breakthrough at every level of our organization, we transformed our culture and introduced an entirely new way of thinking about our future.

Looking back at the late 1990s, the Wrigley Company was at a critical juncture in our history. We were the world's largest manufacturer of chewing gum with annual revenues of $2 billion. We were a recognized leader in the chewing-gum category, but we were not competing outside our niche and we were missing out on key opportunities in the broader confections category.

If we were to strengthen our core chewing-gum business and expand beyond gum, we needed to redefine our vision and transform our organization. Our goal was sustainable, generational growth—and the key to achieving that growth was an improved capacity to innovate at every level. It was vitally important for our company to foster a culture of innovation among our people and to help them understand that innovation is inextricably linked to business growth.

I first met Dr. Bart Sayle in November 2000, when he worked with our leadership group as we developed our vision to change the trajectory of our growth and redefine the scope of our business. He also introduced us to Dr. Surinder Kumar, whom we subsequently invited to become our first chief innovation officer in 2001 to help lead our transformation.

Through their Breakthrough approach to innovation, Bart and Surinder helped us shift from a status quo business approach to a can do corporate culture in which each associate feels empowered and has the ability to impact our future.

Breakthrough helped us:

- listen to our consumers and our own associates
- broaden our strategy based on better consumer insights
- transform the mind-set of our people
- accept, manage, and lead change
- go beyond intentions to actually applying and executing new systems and ideas
- and translate innovations into unique marketable ideas that drive growth

Of course, innovation goes beyond creative product ideas. According to Surinder, "Innovation is the art, science, and discipline of finding, creating, or converting new ideas into business growth." It is a cultural attitude and a way of thinking . . . and it should filter into the way a company recruits, develops, and motivates people, improves processes, structures its organization, *and* develops and launches new products.

Transformational growth also requires more than just innovation. We learned early on that a culture of innovation must be supported by a strong vision, a team-oriented collaborative atmosphere, a passion for understanding consumers, long-term innovation investments, and remarkable people.

One of the most important lessons we learned along the way

was the need to help our people see the future, believe in their abilities to make it happen, and follow through with action.

Nothing has been more rewarding than to see our company growth open the door to the personal growth of our people. The real Breakthrough comes when talented individuals come together to create something extraordinary.

While we have made great progress, our journey is far from over. The legacy of this generation of Wrigley associates will be to leave our organization stronger than it was when we began and poised for sustainable growth for those who follow.

Dr. Bart Sayle and Dr. Surinder Kumar have helped us transform our people, our culture, and our processes, thereby helping us establish a new trajectory for business growth.

—William Wrigley, Jr.

CONTENTS

Foreword   vii

One   THE BREAKTHROUGH JOURNEY   1

Two   THE POWER OF MAGICAL THINKING   21

Three   THE FIVE POWERS   43

Four   EMPOWERING AND LIMITING BELIEFS   65

Five   RED TRAIN, BLUE TRAIN   87

Six   BREAKTHROUGH COMMUNICATIONS   103

Seven   FULL-ON   131

Eight   LINE OF ONE   151

Nine   THE BREAKTHROUGH LEADER   173

Ten   ACHIEVING THE FUTURE   195

Acknowledgments   219

Index   221

CHAPTER ONE

THE BREAKTHROUGH JOURNEY

A hundred years of business success doesn't guarantee the future. For over a century, the Wm. Wrigley Jr. Company has been successfully building its global business and today is recognized as an icon of corporate America. In 2000, however, the growth of the two-billion-dollar company was nowhere as explosive as it once had been. In the United States, sales growth had slowed to a 2 percent annual rate and there was little focus on innovation, with new products contributing approximately 5 percent of total sales. In Europe and Asia, sales growth rates were slightly better at about 5 percent, thanks to more aggressive marketing campaigns and new products launches in those regions, yet the teams themselves operated in silos that stymied knowledge transfer and collaboration across regions and functions. Meanwhile, the energy of the company reflected its sales performance. Wrigley associates around the world had many ideas on how to drive the business to new heights, yet the culture was conservative and risk averse. Managers had become accustomed to funneling most business decisions up to the head of the company with little room for dialogue and debate—in effect, dampening the spirit, passion, and creativity of the people.

The Wrigley company was missing key opportunities to leverage the talent and commitment of its people and this was reflected in the performance of the overall business. But things were about to change. The company had a new CEO, thirty-five-year-old Bill Wrigley, Jr., thrust into early leadership in 1999 after the sudden death of his father, who had run the business for nearly forty years. Although appointed with the full confidence of the board, many others questioned this decision, believing he was too young and inexperienced to take the company in the right direction. In fact, some feared that he'd steer Wrigley the *wrong* way; that he was too much of a maverick, too prone to taking risks; or that he would threaten the status quo that had been successful enough under his father's leadership.

Bill Wrigley, Jr., took over a company in transition. There were many good people, but they were lacking a unified direction, short on inspiration, and not realizing their full potential as a global team.

The Breakthrough Group knew none of this when a call came to our London offices from someone who declined to identify himself. "I'm on the executive team of an American corporation," he said. "I don't want to say who we are right now. We have heard that you have an unusual approach that we may be interested in. Our executive team is flying to Europe for a meeting and I want you to convince me why we should stop in London to pick up the material on your program."

Bart told the mysterious caller enough about what we'd done with companies like British Airways, Procter & Gamble, PepsiCo, and Warner-Lambert to convince the caller to make the stop in England, and we sent someone to the airport runway to meet their company jet with a packet of our materials. As the plane took off, we still had no idea which company had just reached out to us in this most mysterious way.

A few weeks later, the executive from the company called again, identified himself this time, and asked Bart to fly to Chicago to Wrigley headquarters. He wanted Bart to meet first with Wrigley's executive leadership team and then to speak with Bill Wrigley, Jr., the newly appointed CEO.

The two sessions in Chicago could not have been more different. Some of the old guard saw the company as successful enough—as indicated by its gradual (though slow) growth— and weren't willing to believe that major changes to their ongoing business was necessary. Bill Wrigley, Jr., on the other hand, spoke of the need for transformation. He knew that the company had hit a plateau and that five years of low growth could easily lead to a business decline in the future. He sought to accelerate business growth through growing and developing people.

Bill Wrigley, Jr., faced a daunting legacy. His great-grandfather—the consummate salesman—had created the company. His grandfather Philip Wrigley built new production lines and plants to ensure production of high-quality chewing gum at a cost competitors couldn't match. His father, William Wrigley (generally addressed as Mr. Wrigley), became CEO in 1961 and expanded the business by globalizing the company and launching products internationally. Each of these CEOs had accomplished a great deal and carved a strong image of the Wrigley brand.

Bill has a serious commitment to the family heritage, but at the same time, he believed that the company needed to change. He believed that in order to elevate the business, Wrigley needed to inspire and empower everyone in the organization to perform to his or her highest potential. This was a tremendous departure from the past—and an unwelcome departure for several people on his staff.

That Bill was so aware of his company's condition and so open to dramatic change was refreshing. This new leader was already bringing new thinking and new blood into the conservative culture. That many of his people had a resistance to this, however, was to be expected. People needed to have an inspiring vision and to find a way to come together behind a single mission. They needed to unleash the energy that only comes when an entire organization works together. They needed a new destination. They needed a new future.

They now needed to tap into the power of Breakthrough.

The Breakthrough Difference

Breakthrough is a holistic, congruent approach to accelerating personal, professional, and business transformation for growth. It is an approach rooted in human behavior and psychology. At the core of this approach is one fundamental, unwavering philosophy:

To transform the business, you must transform the people;
To build the business, you must build the people;
To grow the business, you must grow the people.

Breakthrough is about creating a culture of growth, innovation, and leadership through personal accountability. We believe it is inarguable that great people do great things and build great businesses. Therefore, the organizations that put a premium on helping their people to reach their fullest potential without limitation are the organizations that experience explosive growth and create a sustainable growth trajectory.

Achieving this power requires extraordinary leadership at every level. Fortunately, this leadership can be learned and translated throughout an organization. A Breakthrough Leader aspires to accomplish great outcomes and inspires his team and those who encounter him to achieve greatness. He creates a Breakthrough organization aligned around clearly specified goals, focused on achieving those goals, supercharged with energy, and acting as a single, invulnerable unit.

Bill Wrigley, Jr., is innately a Breakthrough Leader—though the Wrigley Company was clearly not this type of organization when we first met with them. When charged with the task of helping them, our first step was to bring their top fifty leaders from around the world to Lake Geneva, Wisconsin. Our mission: to give them the tools with which they could create the future.

For three days straight from 7:00 A.M. to midnight, we worked with these executives to draw up a blueprint for the "new" Wrigley. This required finding ways to escape from the past—from the belief that the path they were on was fine and that radical change was unnecessary.

During those intensive sessions, Bill Wrigley, Jr., set a bold aspirational goal: to increase Wrigley revenues from two billion dollars to five billion dollars by 2007. When they heard this for the first time, many of the executives looked stunned. After all, it had taken Wrigley a hundred years to reach a billion dollars in revenues and ten more years to reach two billion. Now the new CEO wanted to make a breakthrough leap to double the business *in seven years*. It was obvious that a number of people in the room didn't believe that such a goal was attainable and felt that buying into this aspiration would only lead to disappointment and heartache. Some quietly expressed concerns that such extraordinary expectations might leak out to the investment community, setting up a situation where Wall Street would punish the company for missing these lofty goals.

What Bill Wrigley, Jr., had in fact done was to challenge the company to follow him and embark on a new trajectory—something far beyond their current, limited growth, business-as-usual trajectory. He saw Wrigley as a Breakthrough company, an organization capable of going where it had never gone before.

Soon after Bill's proclamation, one senior executive stood to ask a question.

"This sounds good," he said, "and I can see ways that we could get there. But how long will it take to get approval on our initiatives?"

Bill Wrigley leapt to his feet and grabbed a microphone.

"You already have the approval!" he said. "That's why you're here. You are the leaders who will set our direction—you don't need to seek approval."

The impact of this statement rippled through the room, hitting some people much more quickly than others. Still, within moments, everyone in the room realized that they'd witnessed a major shift in the Wrigley culture—a shift many had longed for. It was a shift from the safety mind-set of waiting for permission and seeking approval from the CEO, to one in which people empowered themselves, grasped responsibility, and held themselves accountable.

With one intensely powerful statement, Bill Wrigley, Jr., put his company on the Breakthrough path. Going from two billion dollars to five billion dollars in seven years was an unimaginable vision—and yet, by achieving its long-term earnings target of 9 to 11 percent growth each year since then, the Wrigley Company has almost reached its aspiration a year ahead of schedule. If its growth continues at this rate, it will certainly achieve it in 2007.

By tapping into the power of Breakthrough, Wrigley made the inconceivable come to life.

A Breakthrough organization is an express train that creates momentum in ways ordinary organizations can't even imagine. It creates the future by design rather than letting it happen by default. It uses the propulsive energy of insight, inspiration, and intentionality to allow people to reach their fullest potential. It charges everyone within an organization with a sense of mission, a clear direction, and the liberating power of personal accountability. It sets a trajectory for explosive, sustained growth.

Breakthrough is fundamentally about producing results— extraordinary results well beyond what could be predicted by the past or by *business as usual*.

Changing the Concept of Change

Many change experts suggest that it is possible for an organization to perform appreciably better while maintaining its existing framework of thinking and acting. Our experience with Breakthrough is that this notion is difficult to defend. If a company changes its goals without changing the way its people think and approach their missions, it hasn't really changed at all— and the odds of achieving extraordinary results are astronomical. Breakthrough requires people to see things differently, to walk away from old mind-sets that limit what is possible.

We call this limiting mind-set Business as Usual. This is the belief that doing things the way you've always done them guarantees sufficient success. The thinking here is similar to the axiom, "If it ain't broke, don't fix it." However, most Business as Usual companies *are* broken; they simply don't realize it. By taking the safe course, by doing things the way they've always done them, they leave themselves vulnerable to competitors that are more aggressive, and to unexpected changes in the business landscape. Later in this book, we'll talk at length about how the car giant GM fell from its lofty perch; part of it stemmed from Business as Usual thinking. They never anticipated the emergence of foreign competitors with fresher automotive ideas or the sudden surge in gas prices, both of which made these foreign vehicles more attractive than their American counterparts.

Real Breakthrough comes when Business as Usual mind-sets are discarded. This brings us back to the core tenet of Breakthrough: *to build a business, you* must *build the people.* One fundamental component of building the people is changing their mind-sets away from Business as Usual. This means changing what employees believe about the company and what it is possible for the company to achieve. It means changing what they believe about *themselves* and what it is possible for *them* to achieve.

Let's go back to Wrigley again. Before the company could possibly embark on Bill Wrigley, Jr.'s mission of reaching five billion dollars in sales by 2007, the mind-set of its people needed to be changed.

This required identifying all of the baggage that had accumulated over the years that some people within the organization carried around every day and into every meeting. What we found was that the company (like most companies we encounter) had a huge set of limiting beliefs (more on this concept later) that convinced many people within Wrigley that they could only be what they already were. Of course they would find the notion of growing to five billion dollars in seven years inconceivable.

At this point, what we saw was missing for many of these leaders was a critical component in Breakthrough: the ability to think "magically," to see possibilities the way a child sees them— as limitless and filled with potential. Instead, there was pervasive evidence of resigned or cynical thinking—the notion that things simply couldn't be done, that explosive growth was nothing more than a pipe dream. This kind of thinking is a huge impediment to Breakthrough and we knew that it was one of the first things that needed to change if the company was going to realize Bill Wrigley, Jr.'s dreams.

During that first three-day intensive session in Lake Geneva, we took people on a journey into the future to show them that another way of thinking was possible. We dedicated one large ballroom to a simulation of what the future could be. The room contained representatives from each of the company's geographic regions and from each of its functions. We positioned them in different parts of the room and had them role-play with one another, acting out their places in the new five-billion-dollars Wrigley. The goal here was to use a Breakthrough concept known as Destination Technology to help the company imagine a bolder, brighter future. We knew that if these leaders could imagine the five-billion-dollar Wrigley, they'd take the critical first steps in generating that future.

At first, there was little more than controlled chaos in the room. People wanted to put their best efforts into the session, but they didn't really know how. As the simulation continued, however, something shifted. They began exchanging ideas, learning about one another's successes and failures, and—importantly—they began to embrace a shared vision for the company. They recognized this meeting as an opportunity to unleash the talent within themselves and within each of their own organizations to create a new future. They began to sketch out a blueprint for the Breakthrough version of Wrigley and developed detailed plans for putting the organization on an accelerated growth trajectory. They couldn't have anticipated it ahead of time (and, honestly, neither could we) but they were *masters* of Destination Technology—again, these were good ambitious people waiting to unleash the latent potential. Change was happening before our eyes.

This led to Bill Wrigley, Jr.'s dramatic declaration of approval. When it was clear that his message resonated with each of them, he elaborated.

"I trust each and every one of you to do the right thing. I know that you have the best interests of the company in mind. You know what? We are going to make some mistakes; some things will go wrong. It's not easy to change behavior—yet that's what we will do. And I know you will succeed. You can figure out your plans and your actions to deliver the results we need and I will hold you accountable for those results."

The relationship between Wrigley's CEO and its leaders changed in that moment. The executive team had been liberated from the Business as Usual mind-set. Still, there was the very real risk that these people would leave Lake Geneva, go back to their jobs, and settle back into their old ways of thinking. To ensure that the company stayed on the Breakthrough path, a strong and sustainable commitment to delivering this future was required. Therefore, each of the leaders took to the stage and made his or her personal commitment to change and to live the new vision as of that moment. They left that meeting understanding that it was their mission to model the new mind-set, the new language, and the new behavior. They needed to "live the vision." They needed to operate as though Wrigley was already a five-billion-dollar company. They would have to go back home with a five-billion-dollar mind-set; have five-billion-dollar meetings; make five-billion-dollar decisions; and recruit five-billion-dollar professionals.

They needed to live the vision now to lead the change.

Riding the Blue Train

A key component of leading this kind of transformation is evolving the culture into a creative and performance culture. Organizations that are resistant to change tend to act defensively whenever new ideas spring forth. This defensiveness prevents leaps in performance because the people within these organizations tend to be more concerned with guarding turf than gaining new ground. This leads to a seemingly inescapable cycle where organizations waste energy and emotions, accept their limitations, and suppress innovation. This cycle leads to a dramatic decline in personal, professional, and business growth. We call this kind of thinking "Red Train" thinking, for reasons we will explore in chapter Five.

The Breakthrough Leaders we have worked with focus on creating an emotional attachment between employees and their business. They focus on the culture, rather than the results. They focus on people rather than processes and strategies. They know that the results follow as you develop people and create an empowering culture.

Breakthrough espouses a culture that takes risks, generates high positive energy, appreciates the contributions and accomplishments of its people, and learns through challenge, failure, and success. This is a creative culture, a culture dedicated to innovation. This culture leads to a virtual cycle of energy, performance, and achievement leading to accelerated, sustainable growth. We call this aspiring and inspiring culture the Blue Train culture.

The Wrigley executives who attended the Lake Geneva meeting boarded the Blue Train and took it back to their home offices—where they promptly engaged their people to join the journey. They took back the new strategic plan dedicated to reaching five billion dollars and brought it alive for their people. At this point, this strategic plan leapt from the slides of a PowerPoint presentation and turned into a living tool. The leaders broadcast the new plan far and wide to inspire buy-in at every level of the organization.

This is a critical component of Breakthrough. The people within an organization can't ride on the Blue Train with their leaders if they are left unaware of the exciting and energizing grand scheme. Keeping strategy secret or keeping it in the hands of the elite is counterproductive. The only truly effective way to bring a strategy to life is to let everyone on the team know exactly what the strategy is, what it means for them, and how it will be implemented. People have much more to contribute when they see the path, direction, and vision into the future—when they know what they are trying to accomplish as a business and as a company.

At Wrigley, the Breakthrough transformation had immediate effects. The cultural environment within the company started to change. People started to sense possibilities and opportunities. Ideas had always percolated below the surface, but now they were released because management signaled that creative thinking was welcome. People had spent so long with ideas or dreams of what could be, but they believed they couldn't speak up. Now, though, the culture invited it.

The people at Wrigley embraced the Blue Train culture hungrily. They realized that they had the opportunity to accelerate personal and business growth. The company started launching new products and growing dramatically. As the core business prospered, talented outsiders saw the organization as a career destination. High achievers who wanted to make their mark sought to call Wrigley home. Before long, the recruiting agencies started to target Wrigley for its growing talent.

In the Breakthrough Program, we ask participants whether they want to be a passengers or players in their professional lives. Wrigley became populated with far more players than before—the critical mass being those who already worked at the company but who had felt discouraged from being anything but passengers in the past. Breakthrough growth is not a spectator sport. In a remarkably quick period, an astounding cultural evolution took place.

Living the Future Now

Breakthrough isn't simply about explosive growth—it is about explosive growth *over a sustained period*. Breakthrough companies understand that a culture of creativity and innovation requires a consistent willingness to reimagine the future. The Breakthrough strategy promotes continuously raising the bar for people and inspiring them to accomplish incredible outcomes. This might mean a little discomfort for some, but that discomfort is an indication of the Breakthrough trajectory. Breakthrough cannot be reached from inside the comfort zone— that's the Business as Usual trajectory. It requires some degree of uncertainty. In the Breakthrough Program, we implore people to "live the future now." This means projecting an aggressive aspiration, imagining everything required to reach that aspiration, and then setting out with absolute dedication to create that future.

Sometimes that future presents itself in surprising ways. For the Wrigley Company, such was the case on a beautiful, sunny June day in 2002. Bill had invited the entire Executive Leadership Team to his home for a strategic review. The business was doing well. Company performance was ahead of plans. The atmosphere was jovial.

After lunch, Bill excused himself to return a phone call. When he returned, he asked the team to accept an abrupt change in the agenda. "I need to discuss something very confidential with you," he said. "I just got a call from Rick Lenny, CEO of Hershey. The Hershey trust's board of trustees has asked Rick to explore options to sell the Hershey Company. He would like to know if we are interested."

There was a moment of complete silence in the room.

"For a while, we have been analyzing various acquisition options," Bill continued. "Hershey would be a great asset. The timing is a couple of years earlier than our plans but if we are all aligned, I would like to tell Rick that we are interested."

Up to this point, Wrigley had no debt. Hershey was twice the size of Wrigley. Many other companies would be interested in buying that business. The acquisition would be pricey and would require assumption of significant debt on Wrigley's balance sheet. This would change the fundamental capital structure for the shareholders. However, Wrigley was well on its way to building the infrastructure for a much larger company. This was an astounding opportunity to consider; the executive team was aligned and united. All agreed to explore the possible acquisition.

The team approached this prospect with utter dedication. Every single participant in the business analysis and evaluation of the acquisition, due diligence, financing, and all other aspects left no stone unturned. This was an organization living Breakthrough. The energy in the company was at the highest level. Initially, Wrigley's board of directors was cautious, but they approved the pursuit of the acquisition after reviewing the strategic fit for Wrigley's business and witnessing the passion and the commitment of the management team.

Wrigley's bid was selected as the final winning bid. Then new challenges emerged. The attorney general of Pennsylvania, who was planning to run for governor in their upcoming election, leveraged the potential sale of this large local business as a campaign platform, arguing against the sale to preserve local jobs. The Wrigley team did a brilliant job of addressing these and all barriers to the sale with the trustees and everything seemed to be moving forward. They literally had champagne on ice to celebrate the announcement of the acquisition.

And then, with stunning last-minute suddenness, the Hershey trust pulled out. They would not sell the company.

After everything they'd done right, losing at this point could have devastated the Wrigley team. However, the morning after the sale collapsed, Bill Wrigley, Jr., addressed the management group and other associates who had gathered. "You all did a terrific job," he said. "There is no reason to hang our heads.

The only reason ever to hang our heads would be if we did not try. Yes, I am disappointed that we did not get Hershey. But we have learned a lot and we still have the best people. We are confident that we will build our business even without Hershey."

The attempt to acquire Hershey changed the beliefs, confidence, and thinking of those on the acquisition team as well as the entire company. It helped them create a new, even bolder vision of the future.

Bill was thrilled with the way the Wrigley team had created a new Blue Train culture—evidenced so beautifully in the attempt to acquire Hershey. It gave him tremendous confidence that they would indeed reach the goal of five billion dollars in sales by 2007. Still, he knew that he needed everyone to envision an even bolder future if the company was to move with momentum on the Breakthrough trajectory past the five-billion-dollar mark. In March 2003, we brought the top fifty leaders back again for a second Breakthrough Leader Summit. The Wrigley team used this meeting to create a new inflection point for the company and its aspirations. As he gathered his leaders together, Bill told them that from this point forward, Wrigley would think of itself not as a gum company, but as a total confectionery company. Bill knew that the company could not grow as fast or as far by sticking to gum. The total gum market was worth about fifteen billion dollars worldwide. The confectionery market, on the other hand, was at least thirty-five billion dollars.

By using Breakthrough thinking, the "old Wrigley" mind-set had evolved into the "five-billion-dollar Wrigley" mind-set. Now another transformation was required—from the Wrigley Gum Company mind-set to the Wrigley Confectionery Company mind-set. Because of the work that had already been done for the Hershey acquisition attempt, this new transformation occurred rapidly. Wrigley's Executive Leadership Team challenged their people to live the new future, and they embraced the challenge.

This aspiration required new expertise and the development and acquisition of new capability, but once they established an action plan, the Wrigley team moved quickly to live this dramatically different future. Before long, using the skills they mastered in their attempt to buy Hershey, Wrigley made a major acquisition of the Joyco international confectionery business in 2004, followed by purchasing Kraft's iconic confectionery brands in 2005. Wrigley is now a significant player in the confectionery business while maintaining their global leadership in the gum business.

Why Breakthrough Works

Bart built his career by working for fifteen years in corporate environments for companies such as Shell, Price Waterhouse, and Unilever. In 1987 he was assigned the task of determining how to increase Unilever's innovative capabilities across its global business. This assignment gave birth to the Breakthrough approach.

Bart realized that innovation was fundamentally a cultural phenomenon—it emerges from the culture and is controlled by the culture. In fact, the culture—as a set of implicit beliefs, rules, and behaviors—acts as a glass ceiling on any organization's ability to innovate and grow. He invented the Breakthrough process to break through this self-imposed glass ceiling.

He designed Breakthrough to work on a company's culture by working on its individuals. It would start by raising the energy of individuals who would collectively raise the energy of the organization. To unlock any system from its status quo—be it a physical, biological, or cultural system—one first needs to raise its energy. This is its activation energy. Once this is done, one can then start to transform this system of beliefs, rules, and behavior into one that performs at a higher, positive energy level. One can also provide a support system—through leadership, coaching, feedback, and follow-through—that keeps this sustainable.

In those early days, Bart learned that many of the people with whom he worked, as successful as they were in their careers, often had deep feelings of being unfulfilled in some areas of their lives. He set out to invent a process that would start with the whole person, giving people tools and concepts they could use to grow in their personal lives as well as their professional lives. The feedback we get from many of our clients shows that many of them see growth in both arenas.

Wrigley is a remarkable company, but it is not unique in its ability to move from limited aspirations to Breakthrough aspirations. It has been our experience that any organization—of any size—can achieve explosive growth if it dedicates itself to Breakthrough.

What distinguishes Breakthrough from every other business strategy we've seen is the focus on *the individual.* The notion that great people working together toward a common goal do great things and build great businesses is so simple that it is surprising how revolutionary it is.

Our experience shows that, on average, corporations deliver only 60 percent of the financial performance their strategies promise. Most companies are unable to execute and deliver the numbers they've established as targets at the beginning of the year, and there's a gap between strategy and performance. The gap is caused by breakdowns in planning and execution, which most companies try to fill by changing processes, strategy, and people. Other companies adopt a reengineering approach and hire consultants, who come in and dissect the business. Companies who adopt this strategy focus on processes rather than people, and the performance gap remains wide.

Growth is either nonexistent or slower than expected, because the processes and strategies may have changed, but the people are still fundamentally the same.

Breakthrough focuses on building people. When the Breakthrough strategy is applied at the individual level, a transformation begins to take place in the employee and then the work group or team until the entire culture is on a new trajectory. Breakthrough gives people the power and conviction to think differently, creating a new, powerful mind-set to achieve goals and dreams.

In our work with people and organizations, we've seen the rewards of an investment in people, capabilities, and support structures. Investing in people doesn't require significant additional financial resources. It requires being aware and committed enough to unleash the talents, resources, and energy already present within the organization, using those to enhance performance, leadership, collaboration, and innovation. The next step is to bring a clear and focused strategy alive to direct the new energy, talent, and resources outward toward the customer and business growth goals. This process of rapid transformation and innovation gives people the energy and purpose to move powerfully to their next level of performance, and consistently generate success. The Breakthrough trajectory leads to accelerated growth, shareholder value, market share, and profit ability.

The Breakthrough Organization

Companies like Wrigley, Apple Computer, Procter & Gamble, and Southwest Airlines operate in Breakthrough mode by creating business cultures where employees are creative, innovative, inspired, and intentional about what they do. However, more often than not companies strategize on autopilot, by *reacting* to change and market conditions, and by attempting to achieve goals through cost-cutting, head count reduction, or changes in process and strategies.

When we first sat down to contemplate writing a book about the power of Breakthrough we knew it would be a challenge to articulate a business concept based on people instead of processes. What drove us was the success we saw with Breakthrough across varying corporate cultures. We knew that it was an effective business strategy that transcended international boundaries. Breakthrough worked on several continents in many organizations. It had been implemented by Procter & Gamble in China, Russia, and throughout Europe. Everywhere Breakthrough had been deployed, we received feedback from company leaders testifying to the massive change and impact the strategy provided them.

A Breakthrough Company creates a burning desire in employees to make a difference, to become contributors, and to build a business that does the same. When employees are intrinsically motivated by their work and engaged in the company goals, the outcome is accelerated success. This type of culture is a breeding ground for creativity and growth that extends to the customer, and to the world outside the organization. A Breakthrough Company develops employees who understand the importance of building people, and these employees recognize the benefit of a holistic approach to their customers: They know the importance of focusing on the individual customer experience by observing consumer behaviors, listening to their needs, and then innovating *around* those needs. The approach is the same for the employees as it is for consumers—in the end, it's all about creating an emotional attachment that will engage their hearts and minds and make them want to be a part of it.

We live in an era of acceleration, a time when technology,

world markets, economies, and consumer products are rapidly changing. In the past, technological advances occurred at a much slower rate, but today these changes are occurring so rapidly that our lives, business models, and the way we communicate and transact are shifting before us. The Internet has and will continue to transform the way the world does business, and only those companies and individuals that adopt a Breakthrough strategy will be able to keep up. In *The World Is Flat,* author Thomas Friedman writes, "You can flourish in this flat world, but it does take the right imagination and the right motivation."

In this innovation era, Breakthrough leadership is critical to build business cultures that will be able to compete in this fast, flat world. Breakthrough leadership skills can be acquired, and strategies transformed, with a timeless approach that will transcend shifts in market conditions and changing world economies. In the following chapters, we'll talk about how the Breakthrough tools work and we'll show how others have used these tools to deploy the Breakthrough strategy throughout organizations across the globe.

Breakthrough was a profound discovery in our lives. We are delighted now to share that profound discovery in this book.

CHAPTER TWO

THE POWER OF MAGICAL THINKING

In late 1943, Edwin Land was walking hand in hand with his young daughter Jennifer in Santa Fe, New Mexico. They'd decided to vacation there so Land could recuperate from an exhausting bout of work. Land found the walk peaceful and restorative. There was wonderful light, an inch of snow covered the ground, and there was a marvelous smell of pine from the woods. Edwin stopped to take a photograph of his daughter and as he clicked the shutter, Jennifer begged him, "Let me see!" Edwin explained that she couldn't see the picture he'd just taken; she had to wait until the photo was developed.

"Why not now?" asked Jennifer, disappointed.

Why not now? Land thought, feeling a sudden blast of inspiration.

Land took great pride in his belief that nothing was impossible. Could he now apply that thinking to his daughter's question? Could he make his daughter—and all of the other daughters of the world—happy by creating a camera that gave you pictures *instantly*?

Edwin Land pondered this notion as Jennifer and he walked home in the invigorating thin air. By the time they arrived, he'd designed a new camera in his mind (except, as he would later say, for "those few details" that took the next thirty years to perfect). The camera, the film, and the physical chemistry required were so clear in his head that, with growing excitement, he knew that he could build a completely new photography system and change the way the world took pictures.

Land became the inventor of the instant camera and his Polaroid Corporation would become the forerunner and inspiration of innovative corporations of the electronic age. The instant camera was his most famous invention but, from the lab to the boardroom, his innovative genius knew no limits. Over the course of his life, Land won 535 patents, joining Thomas Edison as one of the world's most captivating inventors.

Land's young daughter did not know that what she wanted was "impossible." She did not impose limits of that sort on her thinking and so she asked an innocent question, triggering a chain of events that led to the creation of one of the world's greatest photographic achievements. Fortunately, her question fell on the ears of someone with a sense of wonder even greater than her own. Though he was an adult, Edwin Land understood the Breakthrough value of thinking like a child. He embraced the guiding principle that huge leaps forward can only come when one allows oneself to imagine the "unimaginable." He knew in his heart that what Breakthrough Companies have learned is a key to propulsive growth.

He knew there was unlimited power in Magical Thinking.

The Four Styles of Thinking

The way a person thinks affects his world. It dictates what he sees, how he experiences things, and ultimately, whether he feels successful or not. Of course, one does not think in the same manner all the time. Every individual has patterns of thinking that have been developing since before birth.

As a child, one has a particular style of thinking. As one grows older, this style evolves, due to a combination of neurological development and experience. We have identified four distinct patterns of thinking in the workplace, each with different energies and emotional qualities. These thinking patterns can be highly positive or highly negative, depending on which pattern is involved. These four thinking styles are:

MAGICAL THINKING

Anything is possible.

No limits.

Thinking outside the box.

HEROIC THINKING

I can do anything.

I am invincible.

RESIGNED THINKING

I can't.

I'll see.

I doubt it.

Maybe.

CYNICAL THINKING
Nobody can.
It's impossible.
No possible way.

All four of these styles exist in everyone. Everyone can be a Magical Thinker who generates possibilities and is excited and inspired by the wonders of life. Everyone can be a Heroic Thinker who takes on challenges, makes a difference, and makes things happen in the face of uncertainty or risk. Everyone has some degree of Resigned Thinking that leaves one feeling "stuck" in certain areas of one's life. And everyone has a certain amount of Cynical Thinking when threatened or feeling that a change or a new idea will ultimately lead to loss. It is common for people to vacillate between thinking styles depending on circumstances. One, for instance, might be a Magical Thinker when playing with one's children, yet a Resigned Thinker when one goes to pay the bills an hour later.

However, some people lock into a particular form of thinking. When someone's thinking becomes fixed on one style, it becomes a mind-set. This person now sees life and experiences from one perspective. Understanding and awareness of each of the four thinking styles gives one the power to choose how to think and the ability to break out of a destructive mind-set. We have found that the combination of Magical Thinking and Heroic Actions puts an organization on the Breakthrough path. Adopting this approach, however, requires making a conscious effort to embrace these modes and to eschew the thinking that leads to Business as Usual. Positive thinking styles have the power to transform the energy of a group, organization, and culture—to take them in powerful and previously unimagined directions.

Magical Thinking

Children think magically. Edwin Land's daughter naturally believed that anything was possible. At birth, a child goes from the sheltered existence of the womb into the sensory richness of the world. She arrives ready to take everything in, her mind driven by curiosity and wonder. A newborn's brain is anything but a blank slate. Modern neuroscience has identified rapid brain and sensory development in the womb, leading to sophisticated perceptual organization prior to birth. A baby is born with a brain already 25 percent of its total adult weight. Still, the newborn brain is pure and fresh, untainted by the insecurities, fears, and labels imposed by the adult world. The newborn sees wonder in everything—in the eyes of her mother and father, the vast largeness of a room, the slow circular motion of a ceiling fan. She will find enchantment in rich sensory experiences— new experiences that are already at work shaping the child's world and shaping the child's thinking.

As the child grows, she experiences her world and her life as a time and place of discovery. By the time the child is two, her brain is 75 percent its total adult size. At this age, creativity thrives. The child's work is to play, and as she plays, imagines, and fantasizes, she does all of it in an optimal learning state. Children think magically until around the age of seven. They have new fresh brains and they use them to have new fresh thoughts. A new impulse will create a new neural pathway. It has no familiar, well-used pathways at this point. The child is still building the mental structures she will utilize later in life. This is why children come up with incredible thoughts and ideas that may seem alternately poetic, profound, silly, or amazing to us.

As the child develops, she is also exposed to the notion of "boxes" for the first time. Boxes create boundaries on thinking and ultimately limit the range of imagination. This happens because, as a child grows older, she is exposed to the fears, habits, and beliefs of her parents, siblings, and peers. The parents believe they are protecting the child when they tell her, "Don't do that," or "Don't go there." The parents have experience with the dangers of the world and believe that they can limit these dangers for their children. Slowly, the child adopts her parents' fears and beliefs and quits experimenting. One wall in the box goes up.

In the years to follow, the child's brothers, sisters, grandparents, aunts, uncles, and other members of the family provide their versions of the world filtered through their own fears, beliefs, and perceptions, further limiting possibilities and experimentation. Another wall of the box goes up.

Now the child goes off to school. In school, the child is exposed to the habits, patterns, filters, and fears of her peers (who have brought with them their parents' and siblings' fears and filters) and those of her teachers. This creates the third wall of the box.

The box is complete as the child grows and experiences the unexpected results of some experiments that she tries and is reminded by her friends and work colleagues of the dangers of trying and failing. By the time the child is a grown adult she has built the box of safety within which her thinking is limited to known areas of success. Since this is so much safer than the dangerous areas outside of the box, she tends to stay in this mental comfort zone. Magical Thinking can only be accessed when the adult is unencumbered by the fears and filters created over time, hence the term, "Thinking outside the box." Breakthrough occurs when people realize that their boxes are artificial constructs and that the walls of the box don't really exist.

As we get older, we use our brain less as a creative organ and more as a management/control tool. We tend to use our brain as a data storage and retrieval device rather than as a creative entity. However, we never lose this power of magical thought. We still get in touch with this style of thinking whenever we dream or when we meditate. Whenever we sit enthralled through a movie or lose ourselves in a great book, we activate our natural state of Magical Thinking. Whenever we spend time actively involved with children, we reignite our Magical minds.

The connection between Magical Thinking and Breakthrough is obvious. When one thinks magically, one allows creativity to flow. One allows oneself to imagine the impossible and set a course for achieving it. Had Jennifer Land posed her question to someone less in touch with the power of Magical Thinking, the instant camera might never have existed. However, because her father never lost his ability to think magically—never stopped seeing the world the way a child sees it and believing that anything was possible—he gave birth to a tremendous innovation.

Heroic Thinking

More than six decades ago, Edwin Land said, "If you dream of something worth doing and then simply go to work on it and don't think of the personalities, or the emotional conflicts, or of money, or of family distractions; if you just think of, detail by detail, what you have to do next, it is a wonderful dream even though the end is a long way off, for there are about five thousand steps to be taken before we realize it; and start taking the first ten, and stay making twenty after, it is amazing how quickly you get through the [first] four thousand nine hundred and ninety. The last ten steps you never seem to work out. But you keep coming nearer to giving the world something well worth having."

After imagining the instant photography process that day with his daughter in Santa Fe, it still took Land and his engineers thirty years to perfect and bring the Polaroid SX-70 system into the world. Back in 1943, Land had a clear idea—but the process was virtually impossible. In the face of huge odds, Land set about his task because he knew that his vision was "well worth having." This required creating a new form of photography, devising a new form of film processing, and overcoming myriad roadblocks to mass production. "I had to do what no one else had ever done," Land said. "How else could the impossible be made possible?" To accomplish this bold task, Land tapped into the power of Heroic Thinking.

Heroic Thinking is the dominant mental energy state of people from age seven into their teenage years. This is the time when one embraces superheroes. It is a time of newfound self-awareness, accomplishment, and invincibility. It is a time for exploring the unknown. At around seven years of age, we start to gain a stronger sense of self. At this time we have few, if any, doubts about the world or ourselves. We believe that whatever we want in the future will happen.

When an adult taps into the Heroic Thinking state, he feels unstoppable. The Heroic mentality says, "I *can.*" Adults recapture Heroic Thinking when they compete in sports, embark upon a new project, start a new job, move to a new home, or begin a relationship. During those early and refreshing times of change and possibility, one feels positively heroic. If one experiences success during those early times, one will be inspired to continue to think heroically and achieve more.

Most cultures around the world have the myth or archetype of the hero. A hero is not a warrior. A hero is someone who steps out of the culture and into the unknown (battle, quest, etc.), returns transformed, and through that personal transformation contributes to and transforms the culture.

Great leaders are Heroic Thinkers who model heroic action, creating an empowering culture where anything is possible. These leaders know how to obtain extraordinary and heroic actions from their employees, and to create a culture of people who think heroically. They understand that growth does not just happen naturally—it must be continually energized and fueled. A heroic culture is one where the employees are not fearful of contributing to their highest potential. Individuals and teams are encouraged to perform at the highest level of their potential, and to share information and ideas no matter how impossible they may seem.

Edwin Land was a master at creating a culture of heroic thinking within every organization he touched. This extended beyond the Polaroid Corporation, where he was CEO and Chief Scientist, to the world at large. In his famous "Generation of Greatness" address at M.I.T., Land said, "I believe that each young person is different from any other who has ever lived, as different as his fingerprints; that he could bring to the world a wonderful and special way of solving unsolved problems, that in his special way, he can be great." Historians often cite this address as the inspiration for the individual undergraduate research opportunity course at M.I.T, a course considered to be at the root of the university's development as a highly entrepreneurial institute. Edwin Land challenged students to think Magically and act Heroically—and in so doing, lead the way into the future.

Resigned Thinking

In spite of the inspired work and messages of Edwin Land, instant camera sales peaked in 1978 and began a steady decline after that. New forms of photography began to emerge and the public taste for instant gratification from pictures was replaced by a higher demand for quality and durability of the images they produced (though ultimately a new form of instant gratification— provided by the digital camera—led to an even more dramatic market shift). Polaroid found itself unprepared for this change in the market and stumbled badly.

In 1988, its fortunes rallied temporarily via a huge legal settlement with Kodak. On the heels of this, however, came a hostile takeover bid that sent the company into a tailspin. Polaroid fended off the bid and attempted a new strategy of taking their business global. Unfortunately, the company's competencies clashed with this strategy—they were technically expert, but sorely lacking in first-rate business skills. They ignored big investors and had ugly scenes at shareholder meetings.

When their new strategy failed to turn Polaroid around, business floundered considerably. This led to widespread layoffs and a sense within the company that the future was dim. The process of dealing unsuccessfully with an evolving marketplace shifted Polaroid toward a culture of Resigned Thinking. The employees who kept their jobs now approached the future with the belief that Polaroid was destined to vanish or be consumed in a takeover.

Resigned Thinking is the kind of thinking that leads to giving up, quitting, or not even starting in the first place. When one thinks in a Resigned fashion, one creates inner self-limitations before experiencing any external barriers. Resigned Thinking will occur when someone is conditioned to believe he is not good at something, or that he is incapable. It is learned helplessness.

In the Resigned Thinking state, people think "I can't," rather than "I can." People in Resigned Thinking states are low energy, they are a drain on others, and they fail to think of the options and possibilities needed to get out of trouble or resolve a problem. A company with a Resigned Thinking culture is in grave danger, filled with people who have given up.

In our teens, we start to switch our thinking patterns from Heroic to Resigned as our life experiences give us a different view of the world than the idealistic "everything is possible" view we once possessed. Slowly, we take on messages from our parents, our teachers, our partners, and our employers, that keep us in a Resigned state. These messages ("Be realistic," "It's too risky," "You've got to settle down," "It's time to grow up") are often given with the best of intentions, attempting to protect us from disappointment. However, these messages instead have the opposite desired effect. They lead us to start to doubt our abilities to create what we want in our lives. We decide that we are *stoppable.*

Resigned Thinking focuses on the things one *can't* do. It closes doors. *"I'm no good at math—I'll stay away from any careers that involve it." "I'm not musical—I am never going to play a musical instrument." "I'm not very athletic—I'll avoid sports."* Resigned Thinking closes off possibilities. This is very different from proactively choosing not to do something.

Resigned Thinking often comes when we sense failure. We perceive failure as a loss—something very powerfully negative. When they fail, many people tell themselves, "I'm useless at this," or "I won't do that again." They lose confidence and self-esteem.

More than thirty years ago, the University of Pennsylvania conducted an experiment on dogs. It wouldn't even be permitted today, but it does serve as a powerful illustration of Resigned Thinking at work.

In the experiment, the floor of a room was rigged with metal plates that could give a painful but not lethal electrical shock to the sensitive footpads of a dog. A large button was placed in the room, which the dogs could press with their noses. When a dog pressed the button, the electric charge was turned off. The dogs learned quickly to find the button and turn off the electricity. Each time the electric shock was fired the response time of the dogs got faster until finally the dogs would wait by the button and turn it off immediately.

In the second part of the experiment, a different group of dogs was brought into the room. However, this time when the dogs pressed the button, the electric shock did not turn off. The dogs were shocked, and no matter what they did, the shock remained on. Finally, they simply lay down on the floor and gave up. They became resigned.

During the next phase of the experiment, the room was set up in exactly the same way for both sets of dogs, and the escape button was disabled. In addition, a window was opened, allowing the dogs to jump out to escape the shocks. When the first group of dogs was brought in and the electric charge was turned on, of course the dogs immediately pressed the button. When that did not work, they quickly found the window and jumped out of the room. When the second group was brought in and the electric shock was turned on, not only did they not press the button, but they didn't even try to escape through the window. They simply lay down on the floor and accepted the electric shock. These dogs believed there was no escape from their plight. They were the ultimate resigned thinkers.

Resigned Thinking is the by-product of failure. One fails and believes that this failure is an indication that one's possibilities are limited. However, there is another way to think about failure—as a result one did not intend. In this regard, failure is feedback and it is empowering. Real failure is giving up too soon or being so afraid to fail that one never starts. If one looks at failure as something that teaches, one avoids the depths of Resigned Thinking.

We all know that Thomas Edison invented the electric light-bulb. What many don't know is that he carried out more than a thousand experiments with different materials before achieving his breakthrough. Can you imagine how he felt after 999 experiments without success? The naysayers around him said, "Why bother carrying on—you keep failing, it will never work." However, Edison did not view it as failure. He said, "I haven't failed; I've just succeeded in finding 999 ways how not to do it."

When young children learn to walk, they try to stand, they fall over, and they get bumps and bruises all over. Still, they keep going and one day learn to take a couple of steps without falling. Then they build on this success and are soon not only walking but also running, jumping, and climbing. If they succumbed to Resigned Thinking, they'd never get anywhere.

Going back to our story about Polaroid, the company descended into Resigned Thinking when the rewards from Magical and Heroic Thinking declined. Rather than embracing the challenge as a call for an even higher level of Magical and Heroic Thinking—leading the next wave rather being drowned by it—they essentially gave up. They allowed themselves to believe that they could no longer drive the marketplace. They saw their own irrelevance as being just a matter of time. In so doing, they heralded the end. While Polaroid still exists today, it is an afterthought in the photography universe.

Cynical Thinking

If Magical Thinking is the most empowering form of thinking, Cynical Thinking is the most debilitating. Cynical Thinking is the mental energy state that is anti-change. In the Cynical Thinking style the attitude and belief goes beyond "I can't." The prevailing belief among Cynical Thinkers is "Nobody can." Cynical Thinking is the destroyer of possibilities.

Cynical Thinkers bring low negative energy into a work environment and deplete the energy of a team. They extinguish dreams and dilute passion and inspiration. Being around one can be toxic to one's life and behavior, and it takes strong personal conviction to overcome this attitude in others.

Cynical Thinking is the result of deep-seated past disappointments. To a cynic, the future is highly predictable because it is one of near-certain failure. Cynical Thinkers use phrases like, "What's the point of trying?" or "We've tried that before and it didn't work." Cynics use Cynical Thinking as a way of insulating themselves from failure. If they convince themselves that a project can't succeed, the impact of failure is blunted. Unfortunately, failure is also preordained because a cynical comment is a commitment to nothing—a commitment to being uncommitted. It is not possible to be committed to a project and cynical about it at the same time. If one is truly excited about a project, if one truly believes in it, there's no room for cynicism.

The intense negative power of cynicism pulls people down. Cynics can steal the energy from a meeting or an engagement. Cynical comments can cause others to curb their Magical and Heroic Thinking. Most people have the experience of losing enthusiasm in the face of strong negative energy (e.g., a supervisor throwing cold water on an idea or a colleague putting a damper on a meeting). Unfortunately, certain cultures equate cynicism with intelligence or humor. People try to show how cool, clever, or funny they are by being cynical and sarcastic. This might come off as "worldly," but in fact, cynicism is simply deadly.

There is a clear difference between a cynic and a skeptic. The skeptic is unsure and needs information to become convinced. The cynic is sure and cannot be convinced by further information, no matter how much is provided. Skepticism is healthy and inspires people to defend their positions and ideas, often addressing and solving problems at the same time. On the other hand, cynicism as an automatic response is deeply unhealthy for any business.

Breakthrough is only possible when organizations encourage Magical and Heroic Thinking and curb Resigned and Cynical Thinking. When one is in the midst of an organization, though, it is often difficult to realize that the organization is mired in negative mind-sets. Leaders need to find a way to gain perspective on their own thinking and the impact it has on their companies. This often requires outside help.

This is a place where leaders benefit from external feedback. Most companies have an external board of directors. These independent directors advise the company on multiple areas. Yet few CEOs and business leaders have close personal advisers who can help them with personal introspection, unrealized potential, and avoidance of blind spots. Like all people, leaders become unaware of their filters, fears, and limiting beliefs. In the Breakthrough program, we recommend that they construct a Personal Advisory Board. This board consists of selected independent confidantes who provide candid feedback and advice on what may be limiting the full realization of the leader's personal potential. Remember the essential tenet of Breakthrough: To build the business, you must build the people. This is as true of the leader as it is of anyone within the organization. When a leader uses a Personal Advisory Board to identify areas of Resigned and Cynical Thinking, he grows and the organization grows.

The Magic of Magical Thinking

As we said earlier, every person goes through each of these thinking styles, and most people shift from one to another at various times in their lives or in different elements of their lives (for instance, one might be a Heroic Thinker at the office, but a Resigned Thinker in one's unhealthy marriage). True Breakthrough comes, however, when one regularly applies Magical Thinking. Magical Thinking *creates* magic. It inspires and provokes the generation of new ideas and creative endeavors. Major innovations and big dreams evolve from a burning desire or incurable passion within an individual's mind—in other words, thinking the way a child thinks, believing anything is possible, and asking, "why not?"

When Diane Sawyer recently interviewed Google founders Sergey Brin and Larry Page on national television, Brin and Page attributed their success to something they experienced in childhood. "I went to the Montessori school, and so did he, even though we did not know each other then," Brin said. "It is a school that encourages different ways of viewing things, encouraging the kids to work things out on their own and not accept the status quo." Brin attributed their success to an early emphasis on the elements of Magical Thinking. He and Page created a cutting-edge company and refused to set limits on what they could do. They built a business on information that already existed in the world, and generated nearly all of their revenue (more than three billion dollars in 2004 alone) from the ads on its site—rather than their core business itself. Such a thing was "impossible" on the Internet before them.

A simple, magical thought, can lead to great things. Walt

Disney was another Magical Thinker, who created Mickey Mouse and the Magic Kingdom from his imagination. Disney grew up on a farm in Missouri, and developed a love for drawing, which led to him selling his first sketches door to door to neighbors as a small child. He left for Hollywood when he was twenty-one with forty dollars in his pocket, and today the Walt Disney Company is one of the largest media and entertainment corporations in the world with revenues of over thirty billion dollars.

Magical Thinking can change the way we see the world. In the late nineteenth century, a fourteen-year-old boy from Malaga, Spain, named Pablo Picasso entered La Corunna Arts School. He created sophisticated images that showed a maturity and mastery resembling that of the world's most renowned painters. By the time he was twenty, he'd rejected the limits the art world imposed, and in a tiny art studio on Zurbano Street in Madrid, painted oil on canvas in innovative chromatic colors. He titled one of them *Woman in Blue* and entered it in a contest for the National Art Exhibition. The coloring and style were unusual for the time, and the painting failed (though that painting is now worth millions of dollars).

In 1907, Picasso created his first Breakthrough painting, *Les demoiselles d'Avignon*. It was greeted with shock, horror, and ridicule by the artistic establishment and with wonder and awe by other pioneer artists. Regardless of the response, Picasso did not allow critics or even the other artists of his day to set limits on what he could paint. His conviction began an entire new artistic movement and led him to worldwide fortune and acclaim.

A corporate culture of Magical Thinkers is driven by a Breakthrough leader who encourages and inspires every employee— not just those in R&D or in the creative positions—to embrace innovation and problem-solving passionately. These leaders encourage Magical and Heroic Thinking and suppress Resigned and Cynical Thinking by creating an environment where the former is celebrated.

Magical Thinking—when combined with Heroic Thinking—is Breakthrough Thinking. It creates the sensibility within an organization that great—"even unthinkable"—achievement is always possible. Leaders who understand the value of Magical Thinking and take the steps to instill that thinking within their organizations create the opportunity for breathtaking growth. The people within that organization are charged with a higher level of energy, the kind of energy that comes from knowing that any day can deliver something extraordinary.

Magical Thinking is not a part of any organization's business plan, but this kind of thinking creates the future.

The kind of future Edwin Land created with the instant camera.

The future of staring down "the impossible" and never averting one's eyes.

Putting the Power of Magical Thinking to Work

Breakthrough concepts such as Magical Thinking have helped some of the largest companies in the world achieve new levels of growth. You might be asking yourself, however, "How do I make this work for *my* organization?" Throughout this book, we will end each chapter with a step-by-step process that will help you bring this Breakthrough principle to life in your working environment. These tools are applicable at all levels, whether your organization is a billion-dollar international conglomerate or a local mom-and-pop operation.

In leading your organization toward a culture of Magical Thinking, the first step is to distinguish the four styles of thinking within yourself. When do you think magically? Does this come under particular circumstances, around certain people, or only when business is especially good? Has it been a long time since you can remember thinking Magically in your company? If so, why? Now repeat the questions for the other three forms of thinking. When do you think Heroically? When is your thinking Resigned? When are you Cynical? Can you acknowledge patterns and circumstances that always lead you toward a particular style of thinking?

Once you've identified this for yourself, it is time to share the concepts of the four styles of thinking with your team. Present each of these modes as we've presented them in this chapter. Take note of how various team members respond, as this may be an indication that some of them are stuck in certain mindsets. Now work with the group to generate an example of each type of thinking particular to your organization. Have your colleagues consider the consequences of each style of thinking as it relates specifically to your company.

After this, illustrate the four styles of thinking at work by having team members role-play various styles. Ask four people to run a planning meeting about the future of your company. Ask each of the four to approach the meeting from one of the four particular styles of thinking. If you've observed that a team member seems stuck in a particular mind-set, he is the perfect person to play the role of that style of thinking, as he will gain a dramatic sense of the consequences (alternatively, you could ask that person to role-play the *opposite* thinking style to see how resistant he is to thinking a different way).

Now watch what happens. While the Magical and Heroic thinkers will stress innovation and growth, seeking to engage the entire team in a sense of excitement about the future, the meeting will quickly grind to a halt. If they are playing their roles correctly, the Resigned and Cynical thinkers will suck the energy out of the room. At this point, call the exercise to a stop and ask everyone involved to discuss what happened. Ask them if they want the company to grind down the way the meeting did. Ask them how the meeting would have gone differently if everyone thought Magically or Heroically.

With this powerful example as a model, you can begin to incorporate Magical Thinking into the environment of your organization. Create opportunities for people to employ Magical Thinking. Set dramatic new goals for the company and charge people with the responsibility of finding ways to realize those goals. Encourage people to bring you their most outrageous ideas, letting them know that while you might not utilize every idea, they should be free to come to you with their wildest dreams.

While many people on your team will likely respond very positively to this challenge, others will not. When you present your people with the opportunity to think in a bolder way about the future, be prepared for those who poison the excitement with Resigned and Cynical Thinking. When you hear comments that betray Resigned and Cynical Thinking, confront it with questions like, "How does this comment move us on?" or "What outcomes did you want to accomplish through your comments?" By showing people that this mode of thinking fails to make a contribution—and that you are aware of this—you begin to flip them toward mind-sets that are more productive.

Ultimately, your goal is to create and sustain a culture of Magical Thinking and Heroic actions because this culture is the path to accelerated growth. As a leader, you must be the model of this form of thinking. Monitor yourself constantly for instances where you fall toward more destructive forms of thinking. Meanwhile, continue to make "unreasonable requests" of your people. Let them know that you expect bolder initiatives in the future. Most important, *publicly acknowledge* and encourage any team member's exhibition of Magical or Heroic Thinking. When it becomes clear that this thinking carries rich rewards for the individual and the organization, you will begin to see powerful changes.

CHAPTER THREE

THE FIVE POWERS

When Roger Enrico became president of the U.S. division of Pepsi Cola in 1983, he took the helm of a brand facing enormous challenges. In the cola business, Coca-Cola was the undisputed leader with Pepsi running a distant second in market share. Moreover, even though Coke already had a sizeable lead, they were actually *gaining ground* via the tremendously successful launch of Diet Coke. Pepsi trailed badly in both the regular cola and diet cola categories and the future looked bleak.

Enrico, who'd been with the company for several years prior to becoming president, knew Business as Usual would be a disaster for Pepsi. With the clear intention of capturing additional market share, he spent countless hours talking with industry experts, Pepsi Cola bottlers, company executives, and employees to gather and process information. He incorporated this data into what he already knew about the industry, discussed his insights with a select group of advisers (including then CEO of PepsiCo, Don Kendall), and with his team created a distinct, multilayered action plan. In so doing, he charted a new course of success for his brand and ultimately, for his entire company.

The first step of the process was to acknowledge that he couldn't beat Coke at their own game. Over the course of decades,

Coke had made itself synonymous with cola beverages. Going toe-to-toe with them was a losing proposition. From Enrico's perspective, the key to success was starting a new game that Pepsi *could* win. He decided to target teenagers. After all, they drank more soft drinks than their elders did, and they didn't have decades of brand loyalty to Coke. Enrico with BBDO and Alan Pottash repositioned Pepsi as "the choice of a new generation" via intensely contemporary packaging and marketing. The Pepsi team revolutionized the advertising without losing the legacy of the brand. The message of the new campaign was clear: Coke was a drink for old people; hip youngsters needed their own cola.

Next, the company threw down the "Pepsi Challenge," created by two Pepsi executives, Alan Pottash and Jack Pingle, taking the aggressive step of prompting consumers to try the two colas side by side to decide which really tasted better. This worked brilliantly. In fact, a large number of consumers decided they preferred Pepsi. As a result, the Coca-Cola Company made the inconceivable blunder of reformulating their drink and launching New Coke—easily one of the greatest marketing disasters of the century.

Pepsi was gaining ground on Coke through these bold moves. Still, Enrico realized that it was unrealistic to think Pepsi could ever actually *win* the cola category. In order to achieve substantial growth for Pepsi, Enrico and his team needed to envision a new company, what he called a "total refreshment beverage company." He knew that Coke's flagship brand was unassailable— even with the New Coke bobble. However, he determined that their other soft drink brands were vulnerable. The company started an aggressive campaign of development, codevelopment, cobranding, and acquisition of noncola beverages such as Slice, Diet Mountain Dew, Mug Root Beer, Lipton Iced Tea, Aquafina, Starbucks Frappuccino coffee drink, Tropicana juices, and Gatorade. The upshot was a significant increase in market share for Pepsi across the soft drink business.

How did the Pepsi team gain such headway for their company? By making full use of the Five Powers.

The Breakthrough Potential of Personal Power

In our decades observing Breakthrough leaders, we have seen that they consistently exhibit an inordinate ability to develop insights, act on those insights with unusual commitment and focus, and inspire others to work in a similar mode. We call this set of integrated leadership qualities *Personal Power*.

Personal Power is the ability to turn insight, inspiration, and intention into reality without controlling, manipulating, or dominating others. Breakthrough companies have people with exceptional levels of Personal Power throughout the organization—not only at the top. These people work together as a team toward a common goal, free of debilitating power struggles (Personal Power is not about positional power—title, office location, or job title). People with high levels of Personal Power naturally enroll others in their vision. This creates an organization filled with colleagues engaged in a singular mission, excited about the journey and the outcome, and resistant to Business as Usual thinking.

Personal Power manifests through something that we call the Five Powers. These Powers are:

Insight

Inspiration

Intentionality

Intentional Language

Congruence

Power #1: Insight

Many years after his work at Pepsi Cola beverages, Roger Enrico assumed the responsibility of turning around a stagnating Frito-Lay, PepsiCo's snack food division. Enrico spent six months traveling and talking with key Frito-Lay employees. During this time, he learned that a new, more nimble entrant into the snack business, Anheuser-Busch, was beginning to bite into Frito-Lay's business through better-quality products and better customer service. From his discussions with the key associates and customers of Frito-Lay, Enrico learned many things. He learned that there was a prevailing belief that the quality of Frito-Lay products was inferior to Anheuser-Busch's. He discovered that Frito-Lay salespeople tended to avoid mom-and-pop shops because they could make more money more easily selling to large retailers like Wal-Mart—leaving a significant amount of volume behind in the process. He also found that the larger stores underdisplayed Frito-Lay products, giving undue space to the competition.

Enrico's research led to groundbreaking insights for Frito-Lay, and he used these insights to change the direction of the entire Frito-Lay organization. His first insight was that the company needed to rededicate itself to quality. He delivered a bold pronouncement to his executives: "Make quality a reality." He made it clear that he would not accept the company's being second to anyone in this regard. The company quickly instituted new levels of quality control, formulation, and testing for all Frito-Lay brands.

His second insight was that giving away the mom-and-pop business because it required too much effort was a recipe for

disaster. Ceding market share to Anheuser-Busch in these outlets invited customers to become loyal to a competitor. He
broadened sales coverage to once again include smaller shops
under the rallying cry *"Take back the streets!"*

The sales organization translated that message into a battle cry:

> *Take back the streets; the big streets, the small streets, the
> main streets, and the side streets.*

This battle cry unleashed the energy of the entire sales team
at Frito-Lay. They got more space for Frito-Lay products in the
larger outlets and increased the presence of their products in
the influential small retail shop sector. This brilliant move allowed Frito-Lay to significantly increase its sales and profits and
to reward the salespeople, setting off a virtuous cycle of business growth and sales-force energy.

Roger Enrico used the power of insight—gleaned from six
months spent in the field—to take Frito-Lay to the next level.
His efforts were so successful that Anheuser-Busch ultimately
chose to exit the snack business.

Insight is the integration of multiple segments of information, knowledge, and experience into simple, actionable concepts.
These concepts become apparent when one focuses attention
on one's *inner sight*. Insights come from within and they are trig-
gered by a thought, a memory, a feeling, or an experience that
leads one to access, in new ways, information one already has.

Insights are wake-up calls. When we act on our insights, our
lives are changed. These insights can give us the information we
need to alter or correct our course toward our destination.
There are two types of insights—the "a-ha" insight, and the "uh-
oh" insight. The "ah-ha" insight excites us and inspires us. It pro-

vides a "eureka!" moment where a new idea or a new vision seems to emerge out of our knowledge or experience. This type of insight motivates us into action and new possibilities.

The "uh-oh" insight, on the other hand, literally stops us in our tracks. This is a wake-up call that shows us another view of our reality—what is really going on rather than what we thought was going on. "Uh-oh" insights reveal things about us or our businesses that are not working—the things we need to change. Organizations that fail to pay attention to such insights run a highly increased risk of failure.

Insights drive innovation. An innovator is someone who looks at things everybody else has looked at and sees what nobody has seen. What aids this vision is the ability to integrate disparate observations into powerful new insights. For example, Thomas Edison was a master at reviewing the work of other scientists and integrating those observations into new insights, leading to new inventions. The actual science behind the lightbulb was identified long before Edison, but his insight was needed to develop it in a way the masses could employ.

Good insights come through the conscious or unconscious integration of a lifetime of knowledge and experience. As a person develops more knowledge and experience, he also develops the raw material for stronger and faster insights. Roger Enrico was able to use the power of insight to make breakthroughs at Frito-Lay because he combined his extensive experience with the wealth of knowledge he gained in his fact-finding efforts. He needed to access all of this in a deliberate way in order to accomplish what he did. And his accomplishments were considerable—the total turnaround of his division.

Power #2: Inspiration

Early in his career, Roger Enrico learned the power of combining insights with inspiration. When Enrico was brand manager for Doritos, he received a piece of consumer tracking research that showed that people who tried Nacho Cheese Doritos loved the product and had a high repeat purchase rate. This was the good news. The bad news, however, was that only a small percentage of the marketplace had ever tried them. Enrico knew that Frito-Lay had an excellent product in Nacho Cheese Doritos—the consumer research confirmed this. If he could get more consumers to try it, he'd have a breakout success.

To accomplish this, he believed that he needed to inspire the marketing and sales team to get Nacho Cheese Doritos to consumers to increase product awareness and trial. If he could, he could generate the kind of momentum for the product that would convince retailers to dramatically increase the shelf space they gave the product. Unfortunately, marketing and sales had already blown through their budgets for the year. Manufacturing was the only department that had any money available.

Knowing that his instincts were right, Enrico convinced the head of manufacturing, Jim O'Neal, to spend his entire budget surplus of ten million dollars on delivering free samples of Nacho Cheese Doritos to consumers. This would be a very risky move for both Enrico and O'Neal. There would be no place to hide if this gambit failed to deliver the anticipated results. Still, Enrico pushed forward and the boldness of his vision proved inspirational. The fact that Enrico was willing to bet his career on his insights inspired the entire marketing and sales team. They in turn inspired retailers with their conviction in the potential of the product and the consumer excitement that the giveaway campaign would generate. This resulted in a significant increase in shelf space in stores.

The sales of Nacho Cheese Doritos soared. Many years later, Enrico championed an idea presented by his senior vice president of marketing, Roger Berdusco, and further built on the success of Nacho Cheese Doritos by launching his "Doritos, D-Day" campaign, inspiring all PepsiCo associates to personally hand out samples of a new, improved Doritos product at locations across the country. Doritos is now one of the largest and most profitable brands of Frito-Lay.

Breakthrough leaders like Enrico consistently utilize the Power of Inspiration. Inspiration works because it generates a very powerful form of energy—in both the person offering the inspiration and the person receiving it. This energy can often lead to accomplishments unattainable otherwise. Inspiration appeals to humans on an individual level, at their core, and it transcends personal and professional boundaries. Great leaders know how to inspire their employees at all times, especially when those employees are shifting into negative modes, mind-sets, and thought processes (we'll address this in greater depth when we talk about riding the Blue Train rather than the Red Train).

While insights come from knowledge derived in the past, inspirations are about the future. Inspiration focuses on the excitement of new ideas, generating energy and creativity, and convincing those who slide into a negative mind-set to think positively. Inspiration transforms. Inspiration opens people to new opportunities. As such, it is a personal power tool that can literally breathe meaning and excitement into daily life. A leader who regularly taps into the power of inspiration builds a culture of Magical Thinkers. Such leaders inspire their people to generate new ideas and create new products. This freedom to create generates energy and an ever-escalating creative cycle within the organization.

The inspired nature of Roger Enrico's notions regarding Nacho Cheese Doritos created incredibly positive energy throughout his organization. It created a landslide of consumer passion for a product and—because he was so convincing in expressing his convictions—the entire division lined up behind him to assure long-lasting success. By using the Power of Inspiration to the fullest, Roger Enrico turned Nacho Cheese Doritos into a multibillion-dollar brand.

Power #3: Intentionality

Growing up in the small town of Chisholm, Minnesota, Enrico learned many things from his father, who worked in a smelting factory. He'd often hear his father wonder aloud why management at the factory would not ask employees how things could be improved. "They pay for my muscle," his father said regularly. "They can get my mind and brain for free."

As Enrico progressed in his career, he never forgot that message. Every time he started in a new job, he made sure to spend considerable amounts of time with people at various levels in the company, asking how things could be improved. He met regularly with franchisees who had good manufacturing, sales, and distribution operations. His intention in doing this was to develop a sound business strategy and action plan. Once he developed the strategy, he executed the action plan with the discipline of a military operation and with 100 percent intentionality. Having done all of the groundwork necessary to build the plan correctly, he steadfastly refused to veer from the plan.

As early as 1997, PepsiCo approached the CEO of Quaker Oats

company to acquire the Gatorade business. Every time they tried to purchase it, however, Quaker refused to consider the sale. The research and fieldwork of the PepsiCo team convinced Enrico that Gatorade would be a valuable addition to the PepsiCo beverage division, helping to diversify it beyond cola. Thus convinced, he would not retreat from his intentions. Enrico and his team persistently pursued their objective, eventually buying the entire Quaker Oats company in 2001. This accomplished two objectives concurrently. He added the Gatorade brand to his beverage roster and he kept Quaker Oats from another suitor—Coca-Cola.

Most of us have good intentions. We make resolutions on New Year's Eve to improve our lives. We promise others and ourselves that we will accomplish something we've long discussed. Still, most intentions fail to become reality. Why? Because there is a vast difference between intentions and *intentionality*. Intention is a thought or desire to do something, a promise to act. Intentionality is the thought put into action. It is the combination of intentions and action that leads to a conversion of thought into reality.

Intentionality is one of the Five Powers because it is the process through which one acts on one's intentions with strength and inspiration. When one employs intentionality, one's mind, body, spirit, and actions are all synchronized to work on one's insights. Intentionality produces results.

Most companies spend inordinate time, energy, and resources on developing processes and methods with limited or no attention to intentionality. This is a mistake. Strong intentionality more effectively produces results than great methods or processes. If an individual, employee, or team does not have clear intentions, it does not matter how many methods and processes are available. Failure (or at best, mediocrity) is likely because the primary goal is missing. On the other hand, individuals and teams with strong intentionality continue to search for methods to achieve results or even overcome weaknesses in the method adopted. Because they have their eyes on a clear goal, they can continue to seek that goal regardless of these weaknesses.

From the time he was the head of Pepsi's beverage division, Roger Enrico knew that the company needed to add beverage brands to fight the competition. By being fully intentional—overcoming seemingly insurmountable barriers—Enrico achieved his goal with Gatorade and subsequently with several other important complementary brands including Tropicana. He never lost sight of his goal and he delivered huge growth as a result. PepsiCo's success in the beverage business has continued because Enrico and his team laid the foundation of the "total refreshment beverage company" and the leadership teams of Craig Weatherup and Indira Nooyi ensured continuity.

Power #4: Using Intentional Language

The year was 1988. India had elected a government that believed in protectionism. Foreign companies could only hold a minority share in any business there. Coke opted out of India because the Indian government had the audacity to demand that Coke disclose its secret formula. The general business environment was poor and unemployment was high. GDP was stagnant at best. Indian states in the north and east were rebelling. The affluent northern state of Punjab was seeking independence and had resorted to terrorism. Violence erupted there daily with stories of massacres whipping through the region. India and Pakistan accused each other of collusion with terrorists. There was a very real chance that either a border war or a civil war would erupt at any moment.

The smartest move for any American business seemed to be staying as far from this region as possible—except if, like Roger

Enrico, you knew that bold actions and intentionality are the ways to win against a market leader.

In the midst of this turmoil, the governor of Punjab and the trade minister of India approached Pepsi to ask them to consider building a business in their country. By this time, Enrico had assumed responsibility for the worldwide beverage business for PepsiCo. He had always believed that business growth came with risk, and he knew this was a risky move but one worth taking seriously. You just didn't blithely ignore a market of a billion people when it seeks you out. He called three of his key executives (one of whom was originally from Punjab) to his office and told them that PepsiCo intended to enter this market. "I want you to go to India and find out how we can build a successful business in cooperation with the state government of Punjab," he said.

The three executives spent a week in India. After one executive saw the conditions, he concluded, "Boy, this will be a long walk for a short beer. We will lose our shirts here." The Pepsi executive who was originally from India could not imagine the possibility of building factories in Punjab. "It's too dangerous to even consider sending our people here," he noted.

They returned to the United States convinced that entry into India would be risky at best. "Roger," one stated for the group, "we do not recommend that we do business in India at all, much less in Punjab." They went on to list a variety of barriers to entry and other evidence of unfavorable market conditions. They spoke persuasively and they backed their recommendation with facts. However, they had missed the point.

Enrico listened politely for a few minutes and then interrupted. "When I sent you to India, did I ask you *whether* we should go into India? I am sure I asked you *how* we could go into India and build a successful business. This is a major opportunity and every opportunity comes with risk."

Whether it was clear or not before, it was now abundantly

clear that Enrico was absolutely intentional about getting into India. Enrico's communication left no doubt about his objective. He demanded a plan of action, not explanations or excuses. His message to the executives was that they needed to find ways to manage the risks they had so clearly articulated.

Having committed to entering India in order to gain a competitive advantage versus Coke, Pepsi people worked with strong intentionality to develop and refine a successful business strategy and action plan. It appeared impossible to gain government approval, yet Pepsi people found a way. Doubters said, "You can't make money by selling soda and chips in India." Pepsi honed a model that worked. The government of India insisted on export guarantees to ensure hard currency to pay for Pepsi concentrate. Pepsi worked out a barter system where they exported Indian rice and earned foreign exchange for India. The quality of Indian potatoes was so low that the chips turned out badly. Pepsi taught farmers how to grow the right breed of potatoes. Indian farmers were at first opposed to Pepsi's entry, but soon became strong supporters, holding rallies to support them. Today, PepsiCo has a flourishing beverage and snack business in India.

What Roger Enrico realized when his executives came back from India the first time was that he had not sent them there using Intentional Language. He did not make that mistake a second time. Intentional Language is the power that allows someone to communicate his or her ideas in a way that generates the desired results. This communication comes from a variety of sources: via vocabulary, inflection, body language, even facial expressions. When all of these communication tools are aligned, the message comes through definitively.

Leaders with a strong mastery of the Power of Intentionality use Intentional Language to reinforce commitment and confidence, creating an environment of possibilities and greater probability of success. They avoid negative vocabulary because it has no power and it depletes confidence by creating an environment of fear. Enrico didn't threaten his staff or talk about the dangers of missing this opportunity. He talked about potential and the huge upside of success.

Intentional Language leads to an intentional state. It evokes motivation and energy. Examples of Intentional Language are the phrases "I will" or "I can." These phrases lead to a determined and intentional thinking style. On the other hand, passive words such as *try, hope,* and *if* lead to a resigned thinking style, which lowers energy.

The way one speaks is a form of leadership that constantly affects the state of mind of all in earshot. It is difficult to be inspired by someone who peppers sentences with qualifiers, negative statements, or de-motivating words. A statement like, "If the market doesn't deteriorate, we'll be able to deliver on our financial commitments" is filled with qualifiers that give people a way out. This is not Intentional thinking. Someone using Intentional Language would simply say, "We will deliver on our financial commitments," and leave the escape clauses to others less confident in their powers.

The difference in these two sentences should be obvious. The first says, "Hey, we'll do our best, but we aren't making any promises." The second says, "We'll do whatever it takes to get the job done. We have a mission." Which is more motivating?

The English language includes nearly four thousand words that describe emotional states. Of these, approximately one thousand describe positive emotions; the other three thousand are negative. Is it any wonder people use negative language so often? Someone we work with was constantly feeling anxious and stressed, often more so than was suitable for the circumstances. We listened to her speaking and noticed that she began almost every sentence with, "The problem is . . ." "The problem is the books won't be available until Friday." "The problem is we have to be at the restaurant by eight o'clock." Finally we told her that there was no problem. Whenever she would say, "The problem is . . ." we would ask her what was problematic about what she was saying. Finally she told us that the real problem was her husband. He constantly bombarded her with negative thoughts. She ended up divorcing him, and in the process stopped beginning sentences with, "The problem is . . ." She looks much happier now.

Intentional Language is based on visions of the future and the actions of the present. It includes requests, commitments, intentions, avowals, and affirmations. Going back to Roger Enrico's foray into India, his message—reinforced when the executives returned from their first trip—was completely intentional; Pepsi was going into the Indian market. With that message in hand, his staff knew it was their job to make it happen and that Enrico would brook no excuses.

Power #5: Congruence

Roger Enrico regularly preached that leadership was the most important asset of a company. He believed that leaders acted with courage and conviction and took bold actions. In his famous speech, "Tyrannies of Incrementality," delivered at one of the annual meetings of PepsiCo, Enrico declared that every good leader had the responsibility to develop other great leaders during their tenure in a company and to focus on big initiatives for dramatic results.

A few years later, Enrico asked Paul Russell, PepsiCo's director of executive development, to help recruit university professors and leadership experts to create the "world's leading executive development program." Russell researched the leadership programs at other companies, read books, and talked with experts and PepsiCo executives. After doing extensive research, Russell told Enrico that PepsiCo people did not want academic programs for leadership development; they wanted to learn from somebody who had actually done it. Specifically, they wanted to learn from Roger Enrico himself. The result was a leadership program called "Executive Leadership: Building the Business."

The program starts with a five-day off-site program led by Enrico. For the next ninety days, the participants apply what they learn at this program to business issues and opportunities at PepsiCo. Following this, there is a three-day workshop in which everyone shares his or her insights and experiences. The entire process sends an essential message to the executive team that they can't blame the company's problems on its leaders, because *they* are the leaders.

Enrico believes that building the business is the best outcome of senior leadership development. It develops leaders through experience. The program has been expanded to develop strong functional leaders in areas including marketing, R&D, sales, and manufacturing. Enrico has insisted that a proven leader must head up the leadership development program, and that every leader must invest in developing the next generation of leaders.

In February 2003, Enrico stepped down from PepsiCo's board of directors. However, he has continued to teach the program at his Montana ranch. He has since expanded his teachings to leadership courses at Yale and SMU.

A person with mastery of the power of congruence is an individual whose words and actions are aligned. This is generally known as "walking the talk." These people understand the logic of what they are doing and are emotionally energized by what they are doing. Their heads and hearts are aligned, and their hands and feet follow.

A congruent company is one where all people understand the desired business goals and are emotionally energized by the vision, values, and goals of the company. As a result, the team works together to accomplish those goals. In a business environment, the Power of Congruence manifests itself when everyone in the culture is aligned.

We, in Breakthrough, see the opposite in companies that seek our services. In fact, this is often the reason why we are brought in, though the companies themselves don't know this when they call. Many of these companies post valiant mission statements and cultural contracts that list a set of values, yet the actions of leadership and management contradict those values. Because of this, the company is incongruent.

Leaders of successful companies are congruent individuals and exemplify that congruence for the whole team. They walk the talk. Congruence can't be faked. People in the organization know it when the leader is saying something he or she doesn't really believe. This incongruence shows in the leader's voice, body language, and actions. Imagine a leader who steps up to a podium with no energy. His body is limp and his voice is weak. Yet he announces that business is doing great. He is clearly not congruent and this will be obvious to all in attendance.

When the head of organizational development recommended that Roger Enrico develop PepsiCo's leadership program himself, he understood what we have come to learn in this chapter: Enrico is a leader with a very strong mastery of his Power of Congruence. His words and actions were aligned so well that he could move people to do things they never imagined or never considered possible. Because of this, and because he believed so strongly in the need to have great leaders throughout his organization, there was no one better to create the system to develop those leaders.

The Five Powers and the Breakthrough Organization— Empower vs. Inpower

Breakthrough leaders have strong control of the Five Powers and work to build those powers within the individuals in their organizations. By encouraging people to build and enhance their own personal power, a leader builds the integrity of the entire team, enabling it to run more efficiently and powerfully. Each individual has enhanced inner power, and this translates to an elevated business culture. Employees in this kind of culture no longer feel that they need to be empowered by management; they now have an inner power. We call this *Inpowering*.

Leaders create Inpowerment when they give their people the power to operate within the framework of the mission and tell them what the goal or outcome is without telling them how to accomplish those outcomes. This requires being clear about the goals, success measures, and values within which to operate, while still giving each employee the creative freedom and leeway to make their own decisions.

Inpower is a function of personal accountability. A company that holds its employees personally accountable creates a culture of Intentionality. A manager can inspire, but ultimately the manager has the responsibility to give an assignment to an employee in line with his or her capabilities and create a learning environment for employees to develop stronger capabilities. The ultimate goal of every leader should be to instill the Five Powers in each employee. If every employee has Inpower, the company is on a Breakthrough trajectory.

The Five Powers Build People Who Build Powerful Organizations

In the past, most business power and competitive advantage came from the sheer size of a business, the technology it had acquired, and the markets it dominated. The scale of resources at its command is what gave a company the competitive advantage. Those companies owned the market and dictated trends. But today's playing field is different. The field has been leveled by technology, and the information that was only available to a few is now available to all at a moment's notice. Today, the competitive advantage comes mainly from the strength and quality of the people in an organization and the culture of that organization.

When applied to business, the Five Powers result in true engagement, high performance, and successful results when mind, body, and emotion are integrated and working for maximum creativity and output.

The Five Powers are people builders—tools that can build a company's greatest asset. The steps to Breakthrough involve incorporating each of the Five Powers into a corporate culture, workgroup, or team to enhance effectiveness and creativity. Insights, Inspiration, Intentionality, Intentional Language, and Congruence are the true sources of long-lasting business power.

Putting the Five Powers to Work

As is true with each of the Breakthrough concepts in this book, the first step toward bringing the concept to your organization is to make sure you've embraced it yourself. To become more insightful, train yourself to become more powerful in your awareness and sense of observation. One of the most effective ways to do this is to keep a daily insight journal. Put headers at the top of each page that read "Observations," "Insights," and "Action Plans." At the end of every day, put at least one item in each column. What observations did you make today that taught you something about your organization or your place in the market? What insights did you glean from the day's work, interactions, and experiences? What action can you take from these insights to help your organization move forward? How do these insights make a meaningful difference?

Train your mind to work at the level of insight rather than only at the level of observation. Remember that insight is the integration of multiple segments of information, knowledge, and experience into simple, actionable concepts. Observation is important, but insights get you moving. These insights will lead you naturally toward the second of the Five Powers, Inspiration.

When you've trained yourself as necessary, take this concept to your entire team. Have regular insight generating sessions with them. Encourage them to move from observation to insight just as you have, to share their insights with others, and to build from each other's insights. Get the team thinking this way on a regular basis. Have them come to meetings prepared with their insights and create an environment where they can develop insights together during meetings. Acknowledge and reward this behavior, creating a culture that sustains the development and sharing of insights. Such a culture works with inspiration to open a world of unforeseen growth opportunities.

To develop a higher level of Intentionality within your organization, start by creating a list with your team of all of your ongoing projects and each project's priority level. Once you have this list, review each project and—*honestly*—assess how Intentional you are about getting the results you require from the project. Rate these on a percentage scale with 0 percent being not Intentional at all and 100 percent being totally Intentional.

Now discuss the list with your team. Why is the team more Intentional about some projects than others? What is it about the projects themselves that causes a distinct difference in Intentionality? What can you learn from the team's most Intentional project that will help them increase their Intentionality for the least intentional project?

Look at the projects with the lowest percentages. Is part of the problem that you have not used Intentional language to generate a sense of priority for the project? What is required to raise the percentage close to 100 percent? Can you realistically do this? If the answer is no, or if no one on your team can imagine how to raise the percentage, drop the project. It doesn't help the organization to carry the burden of projects that will never come to fruition.

Now look at the high-percentage projects. For each of these, select a person on your team who has an especially high level of conviction about one of these projects and appoint him or her as the project leader. Put this project on the fast track—using strong Intentional language—with key milestones and progress points.

Making your organization more congruent requires careful observation and the help of outsiders. The first step is to identify whether your company values are in alignment with the behaviors of your people. Do you believe that everyone is operating with the same set of goals and the same level of Intentionality about reaching those goals? Does the outside world agree with you? Use online surveys (or some other survey tool) to learn if your associates, your customers, your suppliers, your shareholders (if applicable), and the general public believe your organization is operating in alignment with your company values. How do your observations match up with the observations of others?

In all likelihood, you're going to find places where the organization is not aligned. In these instances, what are the causes? Have you failed to communicate the company values effectively to every member of your team? Are some of your leaders and managers out of synch with the agreed-upon values? Do what is necessary to change this behavior—even if it means changing the people themselves, should they choose not to come into alignment.

The result of all of these exercises will be a more vibrant organization, one that takes full advantage of the Five Powers to propel the company to greater success.

CHAPTER FOUR

EMPOWERING AND LIMITING BELIEFS

In 1879, Joseph Lister, known as the father of modern antiseptics, created a general antiseptic that had unusual power and effectiveness. He concentrated on the product's germ-killing ability, and since he intended it to be used in a variety of ways, he gave little to no thought to the taste of his invention. His only goal was effectiveness. Sixteen years later, however, Lister's antiseptic—which he called Listerine—gained widespread acceptance among dentists, who marveled at the product's oral care benefits and didn't seem to mind that the stuff tasted awful. The support of dentists drove the product into the general marketplace and Listerine became the first over-the-counter mouthwash sold in the United States.

For more than one hundred years, the product stayed the same. In spite of its unappealing amber color, its dreadful medicinal flavor, and its generic packaging, Listerine remained the gold standard for mouthwashes. In 1985, sales of Listerine reached two hundred million dollars in the United States alone.

Nothing that finds that level of success goes unnoticed by the competition. In response to the obvious market demand, Procter & Gamble launched Scope. Scope was a better-tasting product and was packaged in a more modern and appealing fashion. Over time, Scope ate into Listerine's market dominance. By the 1990s, Scope posed a formidable threat, one that had the potential to make Listerine an also-ran. Warner-Lambert, owners of the Listerine brand, needed to do something to reverse this trend. Extensive market research led them to one bracing conclusion: They needed to make Listerine taste better, while retaining its superior germ-killing properties.

This was a daunting task for Warner-Lambert execs. This product had stayed *exactly the same* for more than a hundred years. As they pondered changes, they found their early work weighed down by a set of beliefs that limited their ability to think constructively. One belief within the Warner-Lambert culture was that if they improved Listerine's flavor, no one would buy it. After all, Listerine was medicine and medicine wasn't supposed to taste good. If they made this change, consumers might believe it wasn't as strong as before. Another belief was that if they altered the packaging of the product, Listerine would lose its identity and sense of heritage. Warner-Lambert believed that customers had come to trust Listerine's generic cardboard box. Yet another belief was that any change in the formulation would endanger Listerine's FDA approval and American Dental Association Seal of Acceptance. On top of all of this, the R&D people had a whopper of a limiting belief: They didn't know *how* to make Listerine taste good. The essential active ingredients had an inherently bad taste.

Meanwhile, Listerine's market share continued to slip. While Warner-Lambert spent valuable time mired in unproductive beliefs, yet another category killer hit the shelves. Pfizer introduced Plax; the launch was so strong that Listerine sales teetered.

For the Warner-Lambert team, and especially the Consumer Products Research and Development division, 1992 was a difficult year. The company had performed a "value-added activity analysis," in effect a reduction of the labor force. They cut approximately 10 percent of the R&D staff through "voluntary retirement" or terminations. Surinder replaced the president of Consumer Products R&D. Surinder knew he needed to do something to shift the culture. He hired the Breakthrough group (he was then unassociated with the organization) to facilitate the process. His goal was to instill confidence and empowering beliefs in R&D, leading them to develop and launch new products for business growth. Understanding Listerine's tenuous place in the market, he targeted that brand as the vehicle through which the division would undergo this transformation.

As a first step, the Breakthrough team gathered a diverse group in a large conference room. This group included a number of Warner-Lambert associates from different areas including R&D, marketing, and other divisions within the corporation as well as their advertising agency, representatives of retailers, and even Listerine consumers.

As the day and the discussions progressed, consumers dispelled some of Warner-Lambert's long-held beliefs. They made it clear that they welcomed a better-tasting Listerine with sleek packaging and multiple flavors. They even presented new ideas to the R&D team about extending the Listerine brand into toothpaste, breath-freshening sprays, mints, and films. Retailers reported that they were not only willing but also eager to have better-tasting Listerine offerings and other new Listerine products.

This was exciting news for Warner-Lambert and the beginning of a shift toward a new set of beliefs. Still, major roadblocks remained. Knowing retailers and consumers would respond to a better-tasting, freshly packaged product was one thing; creating that product was another. To address this, Surinder pulled together a cross-functional team including members of product development, engineering, regulatory, dentists, and packaging.

He asked every member of the team how long it would take to develop a great-tasting Listerine. Out of the twenty-member team, only one person said that it could be done in less than two years. Surinder appointed him as the team leader and offered the team his full support. He made it clear that can-do thinking would drive the R&D division now and in the future.

Eighteen months later, the new Listerine hit the market. It tasted better, it worked just as well, and it still had the ADA seal. Soon thereafter, the same team developed a new plastic package. These initiatives helped Listerine grow at more than double the previous rate and put some distance between itself and the competition. Since then, Warner-Lambert (subsequently acquired by Pfizer) has launched three new flavors of Listerine, as well as Listerine toothpaste and Listerine PocketPaks—a thin film that freshens breath.

A brand on the verge of irrelevance surged ahead of the competition once again—all because of a shift from a culture of limiting beliefs to one of empowering beliefs.

The Two Faces of Belief

Every human has a set of beliefs. Subconsciously, we have beliefs about everything we've ever encountered. These beliefs are shaped and solidified by observations and experiences, and they affect the way we perform in every aspect of our lives, including the workplace. Beliefs aren't simply opinions; they're stronger than opinions because they are supported by evidence a person gains through life experience. Therefore, while some might change an opinion relatively quickly when presented with new or contrary information, most tend to be more steadfast in maintaining old beliefs.

Beliefs live in the unconscious mind. Some beliefs empower

you to accomplish extraordinary goals in life; these are known as *Empowering Beliefs*. Empowering Beliefs motivate and encourage, even during the worst of times. Empowering Beliefs fuel the Breakthrough trajectory to growth. The Warner-Lambert team member who stated his belief that Listerine could be reformulated in less than two years drove that innovation. His beliefs led the team to success.

Conversely, *Limiting Beliefs* compromise the potential of a person. At the corporate level, this weakens the possibilities for the organization, because Limiting Beliefs limit what people can accomplish. Think again about Warner-Lambert and Listerine. The long-held Limiting Beliefs about what the public wanted and about what R&D could accomplish nearly undercut a brand that was a market leader for more than a century.

The Iceberg Model

The iceberg is a useful metaphor for showing how human beings function based on awareness. We know that what we see above the waterline—the tip of the iceberg—is a mere fraction of what exists beneath. In our iceberg model, conscious awareness exists above the waterline. Below the waterline are all of the unconscious things that exist outside of one's awareness—things such as habits, physiology, prejudices, memories, and experiences.

In business, the energy people have is affected dramatically—positively or negatively—by what they carry below the waterline. Beliefs exist below the waterline and are managed by the unconscious. Few people have easy access to their unconscious. Some who have mastered meditation and hypnosis are quite adept, but most are unaware of the habitual patterns, judgments, and prejudices stored in the unconscious. However, uncovering

Iceberg Awareness

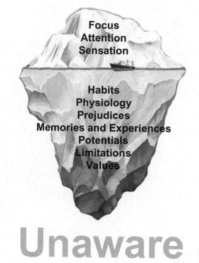

Self-Aware

Focus
Attention
Sensation

Habits
Physiology
Prejudices
Memories and Experiences
Potentials
Limitations
Values

Unaware

Limiting Beliefs within an organization is a key to putting that organization on a Breakthrough trajectory. Once Surinder understood the pervasive Limiting Beliefs running through Warner-Lambert, he was capable of addressing those beliefs head-on and turning them into Empowering Beliefs by underscoring the necessity of and potential for accomplishment.

One can flip from Limiting Beliefs to Empowering Beliefs. In Surinder's case with Warner-Lambert and Listerine, he took the most direct route—he exposed and exploded the negative thinking. When it became clear that his team was holding onto long-held notions—notions that made it impossible to do what was necessary to stay competitive—he used very strong Intentional Language to tell the team that those notions were no longer acceptable. He put the person with the strongest can-do spirit at the head of the operation and through this example led the rest of the team toward a more empowering state of mind.

Filters

The Breakthrough Group had very effectively enrolled and energized the Consumer Products R&D group at Warner-Lambert. Realizing the power of Breakthrough, Surinder next invited the Breakthrough Group to help navigate a joint venture with Glaxo, with the aim of getting the two organizations to work together powerfully, for another project. Warner-Lambert had achieved extraordinary success taking the prescription drug Benadryl over the counter, making it available to consumers through pharmacies and retail stores without prescription. Glaxo had developed the prescription acid-reduction drug Zantac, wanted to take it over the counter, and sought Warner-Lambert's expertise in this arena. The joint venture meant that Warner-Lambert would address the process of FDA approval for Zantac, while Glaxo would market the product. The deal came together at the CEO level, but when it came time to execute the project, there was a great deal of resistance from the lower ranks, especially at Glaxo.

At the time, Surinder was the president of Consumer Products R&D for Warner-Lambert and Mel Goodes, Warner-Lambert's CEO, directed him to spearhead the project along with George Fotiades, the president of Warner-Lambert's Consumer Health Products division. In order to get Zantac approved by the FDA, Warner-Lambert needed the safety and efficacy data of the prescription version of the drug from Glaxo scientists. Surinder's team scheduled meetings between the two companies and that was when the problems began. The marketers and scientists at

Glaxo had built the Zantac brand from scratch and believed they were perfectly capable of getting FDA approval for Zantac without Warner-Lambert's help. Glaxo executives wouldn't return Warner-Lambert's phone calls and something had to be done to open up a dialogue. The Warner-Lambert executives proposed a meeting of both sides at a neutral, off-site location. They suggested that the meeting be facilitated by an independent organization—the Breakthrough Group—and told Glaxo that if after twenty-four hours their team decided they didn't want to continue the discussion, Warner-Lambert would pay for their time and bear all costs associated with Breakthrough. Glaxo reluctantly agreed.

The Breakthrough session with Glaxo kicked off with an informal dinner in a remote conference center in North Carolina. The Glaxo executives included the head of R&D, two executives from clinical and regulatory affairs, the president of the gastrointestinal division, and the executive charged with getting FDA approval of Zantac. When the session began, they were cordial but guarded. There was clearly something going on here, something that needed to be addressed before meaningful work could begin.

After dinner, the Breakthrough Group divided the Glaxo and Warner-Lambert teams into separate rooms. In the Glaxo room, we asked the executives to write their thoughts on an easel board about how they felt the Warner-Lambert people perceived them. In the Warner-Lambert room, we asked the team to write their actual perceptions of the Glaxo employees.

When the teams reconvened, we first posted the Glaxo comments. It quickly became apparent that there were insecurities at play that had created barriers to cooperation. Glaring back from the easel were sentences that said it all:

"These people (the Warner-Lambert team) must think we're idiots."

"They must think we're stupid and don't know the FDA process."

"Warner-Lambert must think our management team doesn't know what we are capable of."

The Warner-Lambert team knew how much Glaxo had accomplished with Zantac and how strong the brand was. They had a great deal of respect for them. As the Breakthrough Group posted the comments from the other room to show what the Warner-Lambert team thought of the Glaxo team, it became obvious the Glaxo perceptions couldn't have been further from the truth.

"These guys know a lot more about Zantac and prescription drugs than we do."

"Will they share their knowledge?"

"They probably think that we are stealing their prized brand."

The dynamics between the two teams changed instantly. The following morning the teams made a fresh start, laughing and talking together over coffee. The outcome of the teamwork between the two organizations led to the successful FDA approval of over-the-counter Zantac.

Once each side understood the filters the other side viewed the project with, progress came quickly.

An individual's filters are the windows of his perception. They color a person's world. We all have them, and they are different for each of us. Most filters are unconscious, and they select the things that we are aware of.

Imagine a person walking down the sidewalk in New York City. How is that person able to walk down that crowded space amidst hundreds of people without hitting anyone? He isn't conscious of avoiding bumping into others, but his unconscious filters everything in and allows him to move fluidly through the crowd without making physical contact. Filters behave this way for all of our actions. Filters color our habits, prejudices, potentials, limitations, values, rules, beliefs, fears, memories, and experiences.

People build their filters based on their experiences. Therefore, an individual's filters are uniquely his. Filters are the reason two people can attend the same meeting or event and come away with a completely different interpretation of it. One might filter the event through fear, while another might filter the same event through an empowering possibility. Each experienced "reality," but of course, that reality comes from the way one envisions the world. The Glaxo executives in the Zantac story filtered their initial responses to the joint venture through the perceived lack of respect the Warner-Lambert team (and Glaxo executive management) had for them. This must have come from some experience within the Glaxo culture that led them to believe the joint venture happened because they couldn't accomplish the task themselves. When the Breakthrough Group made the Glaxo executives aware of the filters they brought to the process, the project could finally move ahead productively.

Filters selectively perceive, delete, generalize, and distort. They allow a person to see what he wants to see. When information comes in, his filters modify the information based on the ideas, values, beliefs, or judgments that support his view of life. The rest is filtered out. Since every person has a unique set of filters, *everyone creates his own experience of reality* and *everyone has his own map of reality*. Awareness of these filters is the first step toward changing their impact. Again, think about how the Glaxo team changed its behavior once they became aware of their filters.

Corporations create their own set of filters from experience. For example, if a company has been unsuccessful in launching new products, people in the company build filters, such as "New products have a very low rate of success," "Since the failure rate is so high, there is no sense in taking the risk," or, "Our core competency is in improving our products, not in developing and launching new products." Such beliefs, subsequently, become self-fulfilling prophecies.

On the other hand, a company that has successfully launched several new products develops a sense of confidence and a belief system driven by this confidence. They say things such as, "New products are the lifeblood of business growth. We must continue to innovate to grow."

At Breakthrough, we believe the leadership team creates, influences, and nurtures the culture. If the leadership team of a company is risk averse, the company will seldom launch or succeed in new product introductions. A company with an entrepreneurial leader who encourages experimentation generally succeeds in launching new products and ventures.

Start-up companies take risks. Large corporations generally become risk averse. The example of Polaroid in chapter Two exemplifies the shift in culture of a start-up company from innovative and entrepreneurial to that of bureaucratic and risk averse. It is worth noting that this shift led to Polaroid's dramatic decline.

There is nothing wrong with filters, unless they limit our potential or adversely affect our perceptions of life. Some filters energize, as in the above example of the filters used by a company successful at new product launches. These filters create a very powerful sense of optimism and Magical Thinking within an organization. However, other filters limit—like the filters that permeate the company with unsuccessful product launches. These filters make failure a foregone conclusion and they are an enormous burden.

Companies develop a set of strategic choices and values. Appropriately designed and communicated, these choices and values serve as excellent filters in making the right business choices. However, conservative choices and values create filters that limit innovation and transformation and put the company on a vicious cycle of negative energy and poor performance.

The Debilitating Effect of Limiting Beliefs

People within companies limit their contributions and growth due to Limiting Beliefs they might have developed at very young age. In Breakthrough programs, we do an exercise called "the Edge" designed to overcome them. In the Edge exercise, participants uncover some of the significant Limiting Beliefs operating in the unconscious, which are holding them back. These beliefs lie below the waterline, and so the mind needs a shift in awareness to reveal them. The Edge takes people to the edge of their comfort zone so that they can peer into this unknown realm of self. For some, it can be a life-altering experience, a true transformation after which they will never be the same again.

In another Breakthrough program with Warner-Lambert, one of the most gifted scientists there (we'll call her Grace) discovered something about herself that literally changed her perspective on her life. During the session, we asked participants to think about the beliefs, values, or other things in their lives that could be holding them back. We asked people to partner with someone in the room and share the information with their partner if they felt comfortable doing so. After Grace did this, she decided that she wanted to share the information with the entire group.

"I grew up in China. I came to the United States for education. I finished my Ph.D in biochemistry. After that, I worked as a postdoctoral research associate in a couple of universities, and for the past few years I have been working at Warner-Lambert.

I believe that I do not have much to contribute to this team, or to society."

Her eyes welled up and she bowed her head.

"I have learned that my mother had two daughters. Of the two, my mother gave *me* away to be raised by my aunt when I was little." Her voice was trembling at this point. "Why would my mother give me away? If I was of any value, my parents would have kept me."

It was evident by her body language that this one belief had affected her entire life. She was a highly gifted scientist who was liked by the entire team and yet she believed that she did not have much to contribute. She was the best scientist at Warner-Lambert and had many patents and publications to her name. However, despite those accomplishments, she still held the Limiting Belief that she wasn't good enough.

Bart encouraged her to think about the other ways she could interpret that belief. His goal was to go to the source of the belief, strip away the meaning Grace gave it, and present her with a new life story based on a new interpretation.

"What is the Chinese philosophy about gifts?" Bart asked.

"They will give only the best," Grace answered quickly, well versed in this cultural tradition.

As the words left her mouth, her expression changed instantly. At that moment, she realized that her family had given the most precious thing they had to an aunt and uncle who could not have children. By honing in on the giving—versus the giving away—she was able to change her thoughts about her life and strip away a Limiting Belief. In subsequent years at Warner-Lambert, Grace published many scientific papers, participated in the development of several technologies and products, and contributed significantly to the business growth. She was already an extraordinarily accomplished individual. With the burden of a particularly onerous Limiting Belief lifted, however, she flew even higher.

When thinking about Limiting Beliefs, it is instructive to consider the gap between adults and children when it comes to learning and accomplishing new things. Adults analyze and think, contemplate and debate. Children just *do*. Adults allow experiences, life filters, fears—and, most important, Limiting Beliefs—to factor into what they do. As we discussed earlier, children haven't learned limits yet and therefore go through early life less concerned with the consequences of failure. Later, the fear of failure prevents a person from stepping out on a limb and taking risks that could lead to extraordinary outcomes. Self-preservation becomes more important than growth and accomplishment.

Limiting Beliefs put people out of touch with the vast resources that exist within themselves. This happens because fear puts up a barrier to those resources. The most common fears are the fears of rejection, loss, being alone, and death.

Interestingly, they link up with smaller fears and can limit one's ability to do new things. An example of this is the common fear of public speaking. When someone says, "I'll die if I have to say something in front of the group," this is only a minor exaggeration. The anxiety and the stress such fear causes in the body are very real, and too much stress over long periods can prove fatal. With the fear of public speaking, underlying core fears—like the fear of rejection—are linked to something simple like speaking in public. The unconscious belief is, "If people make fun of me it will be terrible," which leads to that fear of rejection. None of this exists at a conscious level, but at that moment, the brain equates the possibility of being embarrassed for a few moments with death.

Type I fear is physiological and energizes you into action, like when your life is in danger and you have to respond. If a mugger jumps you on a street corner, you'll respond with Type I fear. Type II fears are different in that they reside in your own mind. Type II fears are psychological; they are fears that you create. Type II fears paralyze.

A common acronym for fear is *F*alse *E*vents *A*ppearing *R*eal. Fear is a belief—an extreme case of a Limiting Belief. It filters how people see the world in dramatic ways. Limiting Beliefs based on fear stop people cold. When these Limiting Beliefs pervade an organization, they can prevent the organization from taking necessary risks and be far more debilitating that the consequences one feared in the first place.

Grace, our scientist friend from Warner-Lambert, feared that the world would ultimately realize—as she believed her mother already did—that she was disposable. In spite of considerable accomplishments, this limited her ability to fulfill her potential. Even people who make huge contributions can feel the debilitating effects of Limiting Beliefs. Any company that rests on its laurels—accepts Business as Usual because of current positive conditions—suffers in some way from Limiting Beliefs. When, as Grace did, those beliefs are stripped away, Breakthrough follows.

The Expansive Value of Empowering Beliefs

The prevailing belief in the pharmaceutical industry has been that it takes billions of dollars in R&D to develop new drugs. Merck, Pfizer, and Bristol Myers Squibb have each spent staggering sums of money with very few, if any, blockbusters.

Most of the pharmaceutical companies in the 1990s believed that the R&D function needed to be kept separate from the rest of the organization, giving them the freedom to explore any areas that energized them. The scientists would explore and

screen hundreds of thousands of compounds for safety and efficacy. Yet, because they had little to no interaction with the
sales and marketing functions, these scientists usually had very
little idea of consumer needs. Because of this, a major proportion of the research these scientists did never saw the light of
the day. Prescription drug margins were high. Companies made
a great deal of money and invested billions in R&D. These ex-
penditures were unfocused and scattered across a multitude of
initiatives.

Mel Goodes, CEO of Warner-Lambert, and Lodewick de Vink,
COO, believed that the people on a great R&D team and the
leadership of that team were as important—if not more—than
dollar investments. They charged their R&D group with empowering beliefs, inspiring them to focus on big ideas and
thinking outside the box. Warner-Lambert's pharmaceutical
unit Parke-Davis used to be one of the biggest drug companies
in the 1950s. By the early nineties, Parke-Davis had become a
minor player. Warner-Lambert did not have enough money to
compete the traditional way with large pharmaceutical companies. It desperately needed to innovate.

Parke-Davis, located in Ann Arbor, Michigan, had been working on a cholesterol-lowering drug for more than nine years.
The Parke-Davis R&D campus was nearly six hundred miles
from the Warner-Lambert headquarters in Morris Plains, New
Jersey. Scientists in Ann Arbor had, at best, limited interaction
with sales and marketing. In 1991, the Parke-Davis scientists
tested one class of compounds called "statins" with a few volun-
teers who had high cholesterol. By this time, a number of large
pharmaceutical companies had already developed and launched
cholesterol-lowering drugs in the statin category. Merck had
Zocor and Bristol had launched Pravacol. The prevailing belief
was that this new compound of Parke-Davis would be lost in the
market as another statin.

Mel Goodes and Lodewick deVink experimented with a new model. They moved a select number of marketing and sales people to Ann Arbor. Parke-Davis researchers Roger Newton and Donald Black worked closely with these marketing executives to focus the funding on their statin. When clinical results came in, it became apparent that Atorvastatin, the active ingredient in this compound, cut cholesterol levels considerably better than Merck's and Bristol's products. The company sold off its generic drug business and toothbrush business to invest in the development and approval of Lipitor. The marketers working with the doctors identified Lipitor as the medicine for rare coronary problems not addressed by other drugs. This teamwork led to the fast-track approval of Lipitor by the FDA.

Warner-Lambert also believed that Pfizer—which already had a number of cardiovascular drugs in the market—had stronger credibility with doctors. Rather than letting this belief limit them, Warner-Lambert decided to give marketing rights of Lipitor to Pfizer. That decision helped build contacts and credibility for Lipitor making it the number-one cholesterol-reducing drug in the world. Its annual sales now exceed ten billion dollars.

Warner-Lambert used the same insights of teamwork between researchers, marketers, and sales people to develop the diabetes drug Rezulin and other prescription drugs with R&D investments that were significantly lower than their competitors. They also developed and used insights to work with companies that had stronger marketing skills and force, rather than limiting the potential of blockbusters by doing all inventing, developing, marketing, and selling within Warner-Lambert.

These developments made the company very attractive to large pharmaceutical companies. This period of extraordinary accomplishment raised the market value of the company severalfold. Eventually, Pfizer bought Warner-Lambert for more than one hundred billion dollars.

By tapping into the creative force of Empowering Beliefs—beliefs that allow us to do extraordinary things in life—Warner-Lambert accomplished things the competition couldn't even imagine.

There's a quote that we use often in the Breakthrough team. It goes, "Whether you believe you can or you believe you cannot—you are right!" Empowering Beliefs have the power to drive success while Limiting Beliefs can leave a person sitting by the side of the road.

Empowering Beliefs have allowed people with limited capabilities or resources to accomplish extraordinary feats. For example, many people with physical handicaps have lived extraordinary lives. One such example is that of Dr. Ronan Tynan of Kilkenny, Ireland, who was born with lower-limb disability. Most people in the little village where he grew up were concerned that Ronan would be unable to earn a living. However, Ronan's mother instilled in him a belief system that he could accomplish anything he chose to do. With his legs amputated below the knees, Ronan went on to win eighteen gold medals at the Paralympics, and became a physician and an accomplished singer of worldwide fame.

Many of our resources such as energy, creativity, potential, and learning reside below the waterline in the unconscious mind. We can access these resources in emergencies, which is why ordinary people can run faster and farther when pursued by dangerous animals, or lift a heavy vehicle when a loved one is in an accident. In everyday life, however, the unconscious resources lie dormant. Empowering Beliefs afford an ongoing way to tap into those resources.

Many exceptional discoveries and inventions have reportedly come from the unconscious. Einstein developed his theory of relativity in a daydream during a boring lecture. It's believed that Thomas Edison slept in his lab because he wanted easy access to his work when he tapped into his subconscious while dreaming.

Limiting Beliefs are driven by fears. Empowering Beliefs are driven by a burning desire to make a difference, a feeling of personal confidence and security. People with Empowering Beliefs have a clear goal and the conviction that they can achieve whatever they choose to. If they do not have resources, they believe that they can obtain those resources. Mistakes and failures don't deter them. Instead, they teach these motivated individuals valuable lessons and help them find paths to success. Remember how Thomas Edison approached his prodigious number of failures before inventing the lightbulb?

What the Warner-Lambert people learned through their experiences with Listerine, Zantac, and Lipitor (among others) was that the binds of Limiting Beliefs are terribly restraining. The culture of an organization literally chokes from the strength of these binds.

When Warner-Lambert addressed their Limiting Beliefs in each of these cases and replaced this thinking with Empowering Beliefs, the results were profound. A Breakthrough organization refuses to succumb to Limiting Beliefs, understanding that explosive growth is only possible if you *believe* it is possible.

Putting Empowering Beliefs to Work

Before you can effectively create a culture of Empowering Beliefs, you first need to identify and remove the Limiting Beliefs that probably pervade your organization. As always, the first step is to start with yourself. As a leader, you need to recognize that most people harbor beliefs that affect how much they can contribute to a company's growth and innovation. Because these beliefs are the result of *individual* experiences, the beliefs themselves are very individual. You won't be able to remove everyone's Limiting Beliefs the same way. The only path to addressing this problem is knowing each of your people. Understand their beliefs, fears, backgrounds, and experiences. To be a good leader, you need to see the members of your team as more than functions and job descriptions. Only then can you help them turn away from Limiting Beliefs and embrace the potential of Empowering Beliefs.

If you know your people well, you can encourage them to take measured risks. Test their limits by giving them assignments that stretch the skills they've already exhibited. If they fail to meet these new objectives, discuss the outcomes with them openly and evenhandedly. Help them to understand that failure is a step toward success, that if they never fail, they can never reach their fullest potential because they never push themselves. Celebrate failure as a learning experience. Remember what Edison said: "I haven't failed; I've just succeeded in finding 999 ways how not to do it."

The most effective way to show your people that failure need not be feared is to walk the talk. Freely and honestly discuss your own failures. Discuss how your own Limiting Beliefs prevented personal growth. Take your own stretch assignments and measured risks. Make yourself the model for an environment free of Limiting Beliefs.

Then you can create an environment rich in Empowering Beliefs. Remember that these, too, are the result of experience—though in this case it is the experience of success and of having conquered tough problems. Again, the first step is to walk the talk. Share your personal experiences and stories of overcoming difficult situations. Model confidence and fearlessness. Show that you have strong Empowering Beliefs about yourself, your people, and the organization.

Again, you need to know your people. If you have a good sense of their capabilities, you can charge them with tasks at which they will be successful. You can give them stretch assignments that take them out of their comfort zones, but not so far that they'll fall on their faces. You can provide personal guidance, support, and encouragement on a customized basis that helps each individual bring out his *individual* Empowering Beliefs.

Most important, celebrate success. This kind of celebration encourages people to reach higher—to believe they can do much more than they ever imagined before.

CHAPTER FIVE

RED TRAIN, BLUE TRAIN

In the late '90s, Durk Jaager, the first non-American CEO of Procter & Gamble, restructured the entire P&G organization. The most significant change he made among many was to create Global Brand Units that would manage and build P&G's brands across the globe. These units corresponded to the category management groups that existed at the company before the reorganization. There was, however, one very significant difference—the GBUs would now manage P&Ls and be financially accountable. This represented a major business and cultural change. For a hundred years, the geographically distributed operating companies had managed P&Ls. As it does in every company, P&L responsibility means power and status. With one decision, the CEO disempowered a large constituency in the organization.

This caused a huge emotional shift in the P&G operating companies. People started jockeying for new positions as the center of power shifted from operating companies to the GBU centers in Cincinnati and Geneva. Because of this change and many others related to the reorganization, star performers started to leave for greener pastures.

At this point, P&G approached the Breakthrough Group to

help reenergize the twelve European companies that were among those affected by the reorganization. We started the program on the shores of Lago Maggiore in Northern Italy at the foot of the Alps, bringing together the central manager and his core leaders from each of these twelve companies.

What we learned quickly was that the tremendous cultural and organizational change had overwhelmed most of these operating companies. The shift of P&L responsibility had left a trail of emotions ranging from feelings of anger and resentment to feelings of betrayal. At some level, this decision and the way it was executed (without a great deal of enrollment or buy-in) had left team members uncommitted to the future—particularly amongst the senior management.

The perception among most participants in our Breakthrough sessions was that the past had been much better than the present was or the future would be. This led to a sense of loss, which permeated the culture. Barriers had been erected between the operating companies and the newly formed GBU power centers. An "us vs. them" mind-set developed on both sides. Now in charge of budgets, the GBUs were sometimes insensitive to the feelings of the newly disenfranchised operating companies and any slight incident was blown out of all proportion as the gossip network moved it around the culture. The upshot was massive resistance to change from within the operating companies, a huge problem for P&G since those operating companies were still responsible for all local activities, from manufacturing through consumer marketing and customer sales.

An enormous shift in thinking was necessary. We needed to find a way to yank these team members from a defensive, destructive, cyclical train of thought—a train we know as the Red Train—and put them on a train of creativity and excitement about change.

We needed to get the P&G team on board the Blue Train.

As Blue as Summer, as Red as an Inferno

Over the course of our work, we have distinguished two basic mind-sets driving individuals and business cultures. Since each involves a cycle of thinking (more on this later), it dawned on us that these mind-sets were similar to toy trains riding on a circular track. We call one mind-set the Blue Train because blue is the color of the sky and the ocean, suggesting abundance and possibility. We call the other the Red Train because red is the color of fire and anger, suggesting resistance and destruction.

People and organizations on the Red Train are defensive, pessimistic, and closed to new ideas. Their energy is negative, they anger easily, and they tend to react in knee-jerk fashion, resistant to anything untried or requiring change. People who work in Red Train companies tend to feel stressed and limited, stuck, blocked, and abused. Many of the people at P&G jumped on the Red Train after the reorganization, feeling that the GBUs curtailed their freedom, sense of empowerment, and ability to grow. They feared the future and felt themselves subject to the whims of a centralized source of power. In such an environment, creativity and innovation took a backseat to concerns about protection.

Unlike people and organizations on the Red Train, those on the Blue Train are creative and optimistic and embrace the opportunities inherent in change. These people tend to love their jobs, are enthusiastic about what they're doing, and feel passionate and inspired about their missions. One of the things we were able to do with the P&G European company in our Breakthrough efforts was to show them how—once they learned to work in alignment with one another—the GBUs actually liberated the individual companies, allowing for greater creativity and faster growth. Once team members understood this, they were able to create a powerful strategy based upon a comprehensive vision of its future global business. They shifted their mind-sets from Red Train to Blue Train, from defensive to creative, from resigned and cynical about the change to magical and heroic about the possibilities, from past-focused to future-focused.

The Red Train: Destination Nowhere

When sweeping and unexpected change came at Procter & Gamble, many people jumped immediately onto the Red Train. Boarding the Red Train is a very natural human function. This behavior is part of our biochemistry. It is, in fact, a component of our survival instinct. People don't become negative, defensive, and withdrawn because they prefer to be this way. They do it because they feel threatened and choose this behavior (often unconsciously) as a way to protect themselves. Primitive man spent a great deal of time on the Red Train because he had to deal constantly with very real life-or-death threats from the elements, dangerous predators, or marauding tribes. As a result, this behavior is "hardwired" into our psychology. These days, we have very little to fear from saber-toothed tigers, but we still have this survival instinct built into our systems. When we face threats to our egos, we respond with this instinct.

The Red Train cycle begins with an event. It can be an event of any size. In fact, little events have a greater likelihood of putting someone on the Red Train because they seem minor and tend to go unnoticed. This event could be a chance meeting, a phone call, or a spontaneous comment from a friend, colleague, or supervisor. As humans, we not only experience events, but we also interpret those events, adding meaning as we do so. We

Defensive Cycle (Red Train)

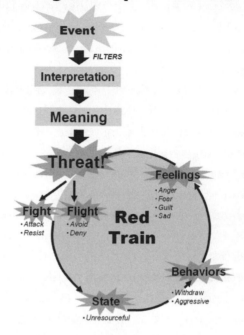

assign this meaning via the experiences we have had in the past. For instance, if someone tells a person she seemed "out of it" during a presentation, she might shrug this off if she knows she had a cold and has a history of making excellent presentations. On the other hand, if she were once fired for doing listless presentations or recently heard the same criticism from her boss, this might make her defensive.

If we interpret an event as dangerous or potentially dangerous, we react by unconsciously activating our fight-or-flight responses. In fight mode, one attacks or resists. For instance, the woman who was told she seemed "out of it" might say something critical about the person who criticized her. In flight mode, one goes into denial or avoidance. In this mode, the same woman might argue that she thought she did a great job in the presentation or simply stay away from the person who criticized her when she gives her next presentation.

What is consistent about either mode is that the person experiencing this response fails to engage with the event. Instead of addressing any real implications of the event, she seeks to protect herself from it.

This reaction is a ticket for the Red Train.

The Red Train destination is a destination to nowhere—a loop of negativity and lack of resourcefulness. People on the Red Train feel anger, fear, guilt, or shame about what they are doing. These people feel upset or overwhelmed by the events in their lives and tend to react instinctually to every new event, rather than thinking the event through. They enter a negative energy state, see *even more* events as *even greater* threats, and begin the loop all over again. Every cycle of this loop increases the intensity of a person's negative state and further drains her energy.

People on the Red Train access a whole suite of defensive behaviors, ranging from passive to hostile. These might include undermining the efforts of others, excessive criticism, blaming, ignoring, withholding energy, approval, or participation, or withdrawing emotionally. They can even include verbal and physical abuse.

Red Train leaders live their lives in a defensive mode. This leads to behaviors like micromanaging, excessive attention to process, and intransigence, and these behaviors tend to depress and inhibit the members of that leader's team. Red Train leaders push their people to "make the numbers" and dole out blame and punishment if it doesn't happen. At the same time, they try to avoid being accountable and responsible—failure is always someone else's fault.

When an organization has a Red Train culture, the effects are, at the very least, nonproductive. They are often disastrous.

Red Train cultures fail to live up to their potential. They fail to conduct business with focus and intentionality. They fail to use the full extent of the talents of their people.

The effect Red Train behavior has on others is profound. It drains people, teams, and organizations of energy, spirit, optimism, and a sense of possibility.

The Blue Train: Destination Anywhere

Bernard Marcus and Arthur Blank faced a crisis that might have crippled many other people. They worked together at the Handy Dan home improvement center and were doing quite well until a corporate raider came along, bought Handy Dan, and fired them. Suddenly, instead of having solid, successful jobs, they faced the specter of unemployment.

Marcus and Blank could have easily fallen into a defensive loop, blaming others for their misfortune and yearning for the past, when they had a great place to work. Instead, they saw their situation as an opportunity. They were free agents; they could do whatever they dreamed of doing—and they decided to make the most of the situation.

They started their own home improvement store, opening their first outlet in Atlanta in 1979. They infused this store with new ideas, providing enormous inventories with a wide array of choices for the consumer while slashing prices as much as 40 percent below those of their competitors. They hired people with the skills to fit various departments in the store and trained them to be customer-oriented.

They called their store Home Depot. By 1981, they had three of them—and sales of seven million dollars—and decided to go public. Within nine years of the "disaster" of being fired, they

Creative Cycle (Blue Train)

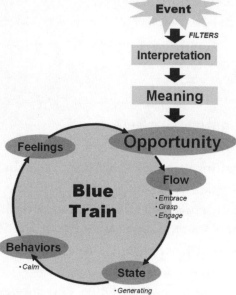

employed more than 150,000 associates and boasted thirty *billion* dollars in sales.

By getting on the Blue Train, they rode off to unimaginable success.

Taking the Blue Train is a different and more creative way to respond to events. Again, the event could be small or big—the response is more important than the event itself. When one looks at any event as an opportunity, one books a ticket on the Blue Train.

People on a Blue Train cycle engage in events, interacting with them and exploring them. They use magical thinking, believing that anything is possible and that they can resolve issues constructively. Let's go back again to that woman whose colleague told her she seemed "out of it" during a presentation. If the woman is on the Blue Train, she'll see this comment as an opportunity to analyze that particular performance. She'll note, perhaps, that she's normally so good at presentations and wonder why she performed differently this time. Was it something about the material she presented? Should she try a fresher approach during her next presentation?

Bernard Marcus and Arthur Blank certainly used Magical Thinking when they dealt with their employment problem by imagining an entirely new kind of home improvement store. They took a significant event in their lives, explored the possibilities, and came away with a Breakthrough solution.

By choosing this approach instead of the defensive approach, one's physiology naturally goes into a "flow" state. In this flow state, one has easier access to more resources and a range of creative behaviors. This tends to build on itself: The more one interprets an event as an opportunity, the more positive energy is increased—and the more positive energy increases, the more one interprets events as opportunities.

One can see this kind of flow during brainstorming sessions at start-ups. There, everyone is engaged in a new idea, excited about the opportunity before them, and willing to be open and flexible about their thoughts. Start-ups tend to be run by Magical Thinkers who set no limits and hold the belief that anything is possible.

The Blue Train cycle is the creative cycle. Even though, like the Red Train, it is a loop, this loop can go anywhere. The Blue Train is a cycle of possibilities. As such, it is expansive, encompassing new opportunities and expanding to create others. People on the Blue Train generate vastly different emotional states than those on the Red Train—states like joy, enthusiasm, motivation, satisfaction, and contentment.

The Five Behaviors of Life on the Blue Train

There are five key behaviors consistent with being on the Blue Train. The first of these is *awareness*. People on the Blue Train live in a state of vivid awareness. They have the presence of mind to step back from an event to analyze how they interpret it, how they react to it, and how they communicate their feelings about it. Awareness keeps people off the Red Train because it prevents them from simply reacting to events instinctually and dealing with them defensively rather than creatively.

The second key behavior is *acceptance*. People on the Blue Train look at a potentially difficult situation and say, "These were the cards I was dealt. What can I do with them? How can I make the most of this?" Acceptance is very different from resignation. When one feels resigned, one surrenders to the situation, essentially letting the situation take control. When one accepts, one acknowledges a situation and then seeks an effective way to deal with the situation. People on the Red Train find acceptance scary, choosing avoidance instead.

The third key behavior is *letting go*. People on the Blue Train let go of old ways of interpreting events when those ways no longer work. The notion of "universal truths" is largely a myth, especially in a world changing as rapidly as ours is. Few ways of looking at things or interpreting things last forever without tweaking. Letting go of these old interpretations and keeping oneself open to new interpretations is Blue Train thinking. Holding fast to a notion simply to prove how right one is, is Red Train thinking.

The fourth key behavior is *taking risks*. Risks are essential to staying on the Blue Train because growth and creativity are the by-products of risk. It is nearly impossible to excel without taking risks. New opportunities are by their nature risky because they take one out of one's comfort zone. When a person moves toward an opportunity, however, one learns something and creates something new. People on the Red Train are risk averse, afraid of making mistakes or being wrong.

The fifth key behavior is *generating*. People on the Blue Train generate many things—energy, ideas, conversations, and possibilities, among others. The nature of creativity is that it generates new things and instills freshness and vibrancy. This behavior is distinctly different from Red Train behavior because people on the Red Train attempt to maintain the status quo and in the process extinguish energy, ideas, conversations, and possibilities.

Blue Train leaders live their lives in the creative mode. They focus on growth and making a difference and they empower others to make decisions. These leaders understand that too much control inhibits results and they relax controls instead. They tend to be open-minded and effective communicators and their team feels comfortable sharing issues and problems with them because team members know that problems will be dealt with constructively. In fact, the Blue Train leader encourages conversation about mistakes because she understands that this offers the opportunity to teach how to learn from those mistakes. The Blue Train leader takes measured risks and happily operates in a stretch zone rather than a comfort zone.

As Bernard Marcus and Arthur Blank learned with Home Depot, the Blue Train can take a person, team, or organization to extraordinary places. Imagine what would have happened to Marcus and Blank—and the business world—if they'd bought a ticket to the Red Train the day they were fired from Handy Dan. The face of home improvement retail would be entirely different today.

Jumping Off the Red Train and Boarding the Blue Train

When people begin to have an awareness of the differences be-tween the Red Train and the Blue Train, they can jump trains and create a more positive working environment. This takes a bit of time and effort. When one is accustomed to Red Train thinking, one can't simply transform to Blue Train thinking instantly. It takes a while for the emotions to catch up. Feelings of anger, fear, or resentment might linger for a period. Remember, emotional responses trigger physical responses in the body; the person who makes the decision to switch to the Blue Train might feel a bit like Jekyll and Hyde for a bit of time. It is decidedly worth it, though.

We have identified a seven-step process that allows people who have spent a long time on the Red Train to switch produc-tively to the Blue Train:

Step 1: Accepting rather than denying.

People get into a defensive cycle in response to events. Many times, these events come with negative energy attached. The Red Train response is to deny the event, to blame the negative components of the event on someone else and to feel victim-ized. Responding with acceptance instead is the path to the Blue Train. Remember, acceptance is not the same thing as res-ignation. Acceptance means acknowledging the event and at-tempting to do something constructive with it.

Step 2: Breaking the pattern.

The Red Train is a destructive loop. Behaviors occur repeatedly and keep a person going around in circles, heading nowhere.

To escape the Red Train, one needs to consciously choose to end the loop. This is a difficult thing to do. Remember, Red Train thinking is a natural instinct. To break a defensive pattern, one needs to convince oneself to reinterpret threats as opportunities. This means moving beyond acceptance to conscious acknowledgement that what once seemed like a threat actually offers the chance to grow.

Step 3: Changing one's interpretation of an event.

People on the Red Train react defensively to challenging events. They interpret these events as threats and seek ways to avoid their reoccurence. Being on the Blue Train requires finding new interpretations for these events. They make the conscious effort to find the opportunity in any situation, regardless of how dire the situation appears on the surface. Remember Bernard Marcus and Arthur Blank of Home Depot? They interpreted job termination as a chance to start something new—and that something new generated more than *thirty billion dollars* in sales.

Step 4: Letting go rather than holding on.

Another trait of people on the Red Train is that they tend to retain the negative energy put out by others. A key step in the transition, therefore, is to learn to let go of this negative energy. Once one has done what one can with a challenging event, one needs to set that event aside. Being defensive about it is counterproductive, as is allowing it to fester.

Step 5: Using one's energy state.

Jumping the Red Train and boarding the Blue Train is as much about changing one's energy state as anything else. People on the Blue Train understand that there are things they can do physically to keep themselves charged with positive energy. Brief brisk walks, exercise, and even conscious breathing can promote positive states.

Step 6: Changing one's focus.

People on the Red Train tend to focus on the problem. People on the Blue Train tend to focus on the solution. Changing this focus opens a world of possibilities. This process involves asking different questions, drilling down to the core of a difficult situation to identify its source. This action changes one's dynamics. Searching for a solution automatically moves the focus off the problem.

Step 7: Taking risks.

People on the Blue Train don't identify strongly with the idea of being right or wrong. The goal is to create, be productive, and seize opportunities. When someone is not afraid to fail, the notion of taking risks seems significantly less daunting. There is of course a difference between taking risks and being reckless, but measured risk—a risk that has a decent chance of a positive outcome—is an essential part of being on the Blue Train and the clearest sign yet that someone is jumping off the Red Train.

Once the people at Procter & Gamble came to see the dark sameness of life on the Red Train, they hopped tracks and never looked back, riding the Blue Train to a dramatic new future. The organization maintained its market position while undergoing tremendous cultural and organizational transformation. Ultimately, they became faster and more entrepreneurial in nature.

The Blue Train took them exactly where they wanted to go—and to places they only dreamed about.

Putting the Blue Train to Work

By this point, you should fully understand the advantages to staying on the Blue Train and avoiding the Red Train. To keep your team riding on the Blue Train, you of course need to make sure you have your own ticket. Remind yourself daily how energizing it feels to be in this creative cycle. At the same time, remind yourself how debilitating negativity and defensiveness are. Remember that it is not the event that boards you onto the Red Train, but your interpretation of the event and your subsequent reaction.

Put this to use constantly. When any event triggers a negative reaction in you, don't react outwardly immediately. Stop and think before speaking or acting. Don't allow your response to put others on the Red Train. Recall a previous experience of reacting negatively and the results you got from that reaction. Surely, this reaction did some damage. Use the lessons of that experience to curb your impulses.

The key to staying off the Red Train is understanding that a defensive or negative reaction is *only one interpretation* of an event. You can interpret nearly every event in a more empowering way. Remember how Bernard Marcus and Arthur Blank interpreted being fired. Go back to your own experience of "turning lemons into lemonade." When did you take a negative experience and turn it into a positive one by thinking creatively? How can you apply that form of thinking to your current situation? If you find yourself ready to board the Red Train, stop, rethink, reinterpret, and change your reaction. If you let the Red Train pass, the Blue Train will pull into the station right behind it.

Discuss these two cycles with your team. Have them imagine scenarios where a negative event occurs and have them role-

play a Red Train response and a Blue Train response. Videotape these different responses. When the exercise is complete,
show the team the videotape, and ask them to analyze reactions,
behaviors, body language, emotions, and levels of energy. This
very powerful visual demonstration will underscore the profound differences between Red Train thinking and Blue Train
thinking and drive the point home that the Blue Train is the
only train that takes the company where you want it to go.

Once your people see this for themselves, they will be ready
for the seven-step "flipping" process we described earlier in this
chapter. With practice, they will become adept at jumping from
Red Train behaviors to Blue Train behaviors instantly.

CHAPTER SIX

BREAKTHROUGH COMMUNICATIONS

Communication is essential for anything we want to accomplish in business and life. Effective communication enrolls others. It moves teams from ideas to actions, and actions to results. The natural ability to communicate effectively is a rare and precious gift. However, anyone can learn to do it by utilizing the five tools of Breakthrough Communications: Power Listening, the Feedback Frame, Powerful Conversations, Background Conversations, and Gossiping Success.

Most people believe they are already good communicators. They've reached a point in their lives where they've been promoted, given several successful presentations, sold to customers, and communicated with colleagues. Someone with this level of experience probably is a *good* communicator—but the odds are he is not a *great* communicator.

In the Breakthrough program, we teach executives how to be extraordinary communicators. As we've said before, Breakthrough Leadership is a holistic process that involves building the people in order to build the business. In order to build people, the leader absolutely must be able to communicate openly and fluidly with the members of his organization.

When one focuses on people within one's business, one becomes more interested in people in general, their intrinsic desires, and their development and growth. One learns to understand their unconscious drivers and motivations and how to work with different personality types. If one lives in Breakthrough, one becomes aware of the things that are usually unseen, and utilizes the tools, skills, and traits available in the conscious and unconscious to become a more effective leader and communicator.

The First Breakthrough Communication Tool: Power Listening

Great leaders and communicators view listening as a skill. They work on this skill continuously, and communicate using Power Listening as a tool. Power Listening is an enhanced, active state of listening.

Most people view listening as a passive activity. They do it while reading a magazine or looking around the room at others. Even when a person listens while maintaining eye contact, his thoughts are usually engaged in something else. People listen and think at the same time, formulating a response to what the other person is saying or filtering out any information they feel is irrelevant.

Habitual listening is a passive pattern that is actually not effective listening at all. While one person is talking, the other is thinking backwards (to memories, scenarios, data that can support a particular view) or forward (to the things that need to be accomplished once the conversation is over).

Power Listening, however, is active and requires effort, self-awareness, and practice. It is a potent tool, because it allows a person to gain more insight and greater and untainted information. It generates more possibilities and provides an edge over those who don't use it.

Part of what leads to habitual listening is the belief that one already knows what the speaker is going to say. What we already know acts like a filter, an unconscious reaction that affects our ability to listen. What we already know prevents us from seeing things from a new perspective, from learning something truly new. As incongruous as it might seem, in general, it is the novice who is more open to learning than the expert.

We're reminded of a story about a Zen master and the university professor who came to learn about Zen. It was obvious to the master from the start of the conversation that the professor was not so much interested in learning as he was in impressing the master with his own opinions and knowledge. The master listened patiently and finally suggested they have tea. The master poured his visitor's cup full and then kept on pouring. The professor watched the cup overflowing until he could no longer restrain himself. He said, "The cup is overfull; no more will go in." In response, the master said, "Like this cup, you are full of your own opinions and speculations. How can I show you Zen unless you first empty your cup?"

The most disruptive barrier to Power Listening is the distraction of the inner voice. The inner voice asks questions and then answers them, makes judgments on what the other person is saying, formulates responses, and creates a to-do list based on what it is hearing. It's easy to spot when a person is listening to his inner voice instead of the speaker because his eyes, words, or body language give him away. He's gazing at the middle distance, responding with nonsequiturs, or looking as though he feels restrained by the conversation. If called on this, he'd probably be defensive about it (and possibly board the Red Train) because of his low level of awareness—people who are not good listeners rarely realize it.

All people have an inner voice that generates commentary, criticizes what the speaker is saying, or even comments on the speaker's shoes or wardrobe. Sometimes the inner voice is listening with the aim of interrupting as soon as the speaker takes a breath. People overly focused on their inner voices tend to consider listening simply to be a chore to be endured before speaking.

The first step toward enhancing listening skills is to be aware of the inner voice. A Power Listener recognizes the radio commentator inside his head and turns down the volume. The second step is to develop an awareness of outside distractions. Imagine sitting in a restaurant at a table by a pair of swinging double doors that lead to the kitchen. Every time the waiter goes through the double doors, the background noise from the kitchen increases. The Power Listener learns to ignore this noise and to focus exclusively on the speaker.

We tend to tailor our speech to the listener. If we know that someone isn't really listening to us, we become cautious and we will not give the listener as much information. If we think the listener has a low attention span, we will hold back information that's too important to us, or too complex to discuss and go to someone else with it instead. Being a habitual listener is therefore a high-risk proposition, as the behavior can actually drive someone to the competition.

Listening well is an active process that involves all of our inner and outer senses. The Power Listener wants to catch every nuance of the speaker's communication. The Power Listener gives the gift of their full attention, giving the speaker the space to express himself. To listen powerfully, we need to pay less attention to our inner interruptions and focus instead on the conversation.

Understanding communication styles is an important aspect of Power Listening. Some people have a "get-to-the-point" style of listening and communicating, using as few words as possible to communicate only the most essential information. They think and talk linearly—in a straight line, the fastest way to get to the point.

Detail people, on the other hand, want to know all the details and often communicate all the details. They adopt a story-telling style, where the story spirals and weaves a vision or picture with their words. In this style of communication, the person shares an experience, using descriptive language, stories, or metaphors. Often they ask many questions. The journey of their conversation is more like a spiral.

When someone with a "straight-line" communication style converses with someone with a "spiral" communication style, communications can be frustrating for both. Understanding this—and understanding that one might need to adapt one's preferred way of conveying and receiving information for a particular audience—helps make a person a better communicator.

Learning this new way to listen is transformational. By using Power Listening in the workplace, one builds stronger and deeper rapport among a team, enabling them to build stronger trust levels and take greater risks.

The Second Breakthrough Communication Tool: The Feedback Frame

Powerful feedback is essential for growth and learning. As leaders, it allows us to see ourselves as others really see us. It allows us to "get real" about the impact our leadership style—our behavior and our communication—has on our people. Feedback can help us to recognize our blind spots and come face to face with our real strengths and weaknesses. Feedback can wake us up so that we begin to notice what we are doing (or not doing) that makes us less effective, allowing us to start the process of changing it.

Powerful feedback is meaningful feedback—it is feedback that makes a difference. Giving and receiving honest feedback can be perceived as embarrassing or threatening or painful. Because of this, honest, meaningful, powerful feedback is often seen as a risk better avoided. Instead, people play it safe, telling others what they want to hear. This, of course, is inauthentic and ineffective feedback.

Few are trained or educated in giving feedback. It therefore often comes across clumsily as criticism. At the same time, few are trained to *receive* feedback, instead interpreting it as mere criticism, getting upset and angry along the way. We react emotionally and take the perceived criticism personally, failing to hear the nuggets of gold hidden in the message, which could help us improve.

Great leaders develop feedback skills that incorporate the Five Powers of Insights, Inspiration, Intention, Language, and Congruence. They use the Five Powers to give constructive feedback without controlling, manipulating, or dominating the feedback or the other person. Breakthrough leaders use feedback to build stronger people, and stronger organizations.

Feedback often comes in a "feedback sandwich," consisting of two slices of "I like this but . . ." and a very thin layer of meat. Most people view feedback—both giving it and receiving it—as an uncomfortable process. Therefore, it is either given well and received poorly, or given poorly and received poorly. Coaching team members to view feedback as a growth tool is a critical and valuable component of Breakthrough communications.

Breakthrough has developed a powerful framework for receiving authentic, honest feedback in a much more effective way. It is simple yet powerful and can be used in the variety of situations where feedback is required. It is called the Feedback Frame and chunks the information you want to feed back into four areas:

The first frame—"What Inspires?"—compels the person offering feedback to express what it is about the situation, person, or presentation that is inspiring. This demands honesty and authenticity as well as generosity. It's possible that one might find nothing inspiring. This is an important thing to recognize,

Feedback Frame

What Inspires? What Works?	What is not Working Yet?
What's Possible?	What's Missing?

though not verbalize, since this could very easily have to do with the views, beliefs, values, or judgments of the person offering the feedback. These need to be set aside in order to deliver effective, meaningful feedback.

Also in the first frame—"What Works?"—requires looking closely at the situation to identify what part of it succeeds. Again, it is important to be aware of one's own filters when doing this analysis. The feedback must always be about the project at hand.

The second frame—"What's Not Working Yet?"—needs to be specific and actionable. Clarity is essential here. Unclear feedback in this frame makes it difficult for the recipient to do anything with the information. As with the other frames, one must be cognizant of one's own filters. The key word here is *yet* because even though we are communicating all the things we believe are not working about the person's behavior or the project, using *yet* sends the message that we assume that at some future time it *will* be working.

The third frame—"What's Missing?"—addresses one's perception of what is missing from the project or the performance. This is probably the most important question to ask and answer in a feedback situation. The key here is offering observations about the things that are missing *that would make a difference.* It is not helpful to include an exhaustive list that includes everything and anything.

The fourth frame—"What's Possible?"—offers the opportunity to be creative while giving feedback. The object here is to look at the bigger picture to generate new possibilities that will lead to powerful results. Here is a chance to provide some ideas and solutions to the areas identified in "what's not working yet?" and "what's missing?" Because the "what's possible?" is the last area in the sequence, it leaves both giver and receiver in a conversation where they are generating possibilities.

Feedback is best given by setting up what we call a "Feedback Conversation"—as it implies this is a two-way dialogue and the meeting of two equals (or two equal parties) for a conversation about improving performance (or quality, etc.). This conversation begins with the giver asking permission to give feedback to the receiver, as doing so makes it likely that the receiver will be less defensive about what he hears.

The intention of feedback is to add value to the person or project. It is therefore important that one "owns" the feedback one offers. Using the words *I* and *me* (as in "I believe this is not working yet" or "For me, there are some things missing") bolsters this sense of ownership. In addition, one must always re-member to separate the person from the behavior. This staves off defensiveness. Good feedback is not about personalities or personal qualities. In addition, specificity and clarity are pre-mium, as these allow the receiver to clearly identify the prob-lem or opportunity.

Tone is also extremely important. Feedback should be deliv-ered in a calm, detached way—observation of the facts without judgment, anger, or disappointment. It needs to be delivered in the spirit of coaching and support—especially if the feed-back is negative—so the receiver can put both the positives and the negatives into the context of their own growth, develop-ment, and learning. Effective feedback always preserves the re-ceiver's self-esteem.

Powerful feedback gives and receives relevant information in a constructive way. Timing is important for constructive and positive feedback. Six months into a project is far too late to tell someone there was something missing from his or her initial project proposal. Timely feedback allows the recipient to make the best use of the information.

The Feedback Frame is an enormously useful tool for per-formance coaching, appraisals, job evaluation, recruiting, team building, conflict resolution, and evaluating new product ideas and concepts. We coach the executives we work with to use the Feedback Frame when working with their teams and colleagues, and even to keep it in mind before a presentation.

Bart recalls a dramatic experience with the Feedback Frame that illustrated how valuable it can be:

> We were working with the Guinness Company just before they merged with Grand Metropolitan to become Diageo. I had been working with Tony Greener and the executive board on their next five-year vision and strategy. It was a

tremendous vision that would build a business of global power brands. We had presented this vision to the top two hundred senior managers of the company and they were all inspired about their future. Now they decided on a high-risk action—to present the vision to a select group of London's City analysts (the London equivalent of Wall Street's analysts— Guinness was on the London Stock Exchange).

The day came and we faced a stern-faced group of analysts. There wasn't a single smiling face—no one giving any emotion away. The exec board was anxious yet eager to get it over. We wanted honest feedback from the analysts and it was my job to get that feedback.

The board gave their presentation. It started in the auditorium on PowerPoint and it felt dry and uninspiring— because we had planned it that way. After twenty minutes, Tony Greener stopped in mid-sentence and said to the audience, "Up to now we've been telling you about what we are going to do—and you look bored. Instead, you need to experience what we are going to do. Will you join me and come this way?"

At that, the side doors opened and the audience followed Greener down a dimly lit corridor from the current reality to the future. We went to a stage set designed to resemble New Year's Eve five years on. Actors simulated what the bars, clubs, and restaurants would look like and, more important, what the Guinness brands and new products would look like. Yes, it was pure theater but now people could experience what the vision would look like, sound like, and feel like— even what it might taste like!

Back from the future, we assembled again in the auditorium. The analysts who had been surprised, delighted, and entertained by their journey into Guinness's future once again had their poker faces on. It was time for feedback . . .

I started by explaining how we would do the feedback and explained each of the five chunks. I then started the feedback session itself. With the exec board standing on the stage behind me, I asked, "What inspires you about the Guinness five-year vision and strategy?" No one spoke, no one raised a hand, and no one flinched.

I decided to move on into the more specific diagnostics. "So, could you tell me what's working for you in the Guinness vision and strategy?" Nothing. I stared into a sea of expressionless faces. The silence was total. I felt the sweat starting to collect on the back of my neck. I could feel the apprehension of the Guinness exec board.

I went to the third frame. "What's not working yet?" I asked tentatively.

The hands shot up!

I pointed to one of the analysts and he started to list the things not working. We couldn't really hear him on the stage, so I asked him to wait until a microphone got to him. When it did, I asked him to stand. This was intentional because I wanted him to own his feedback in front of the entire crowd. As he stood and spoke into the microphone, we just listened and the exec board took notes. I had already coached them not to interrupt and not to defend or justify. They could ask for clarification, but nothing more.

The analyst finished and was just about to sit down when I said to him, "Before you sit down, can I ask you what inspired you about the vision?" He looked blank for a moment and then said, "Of course." He looked down at some notes he'd taken and said he was inspired by the boldness of the vision and the courage of the exec board to present it in this way to this audience. I asked him to tell us what specifically was working for him about this vision. By this point, he was comfortable and in flow and he listed a number of things that he felt worked. Finally, I asked him, "So building on what you have seen and experienced, what's possible for Guinness with such a vision and strategy?" Now he was generating ideas for us, interacting with the team—and smiling. He sat down to a wave of applause.

The ice had broken, a forest of hands went up, and seemingly everyone wanted to contribute their feedback. It was a great day for the Guinness Company, for the exec board, and for me (I even got a new client from it!).

I have a suspicion it was also a great meeting for many of the analysts.

The Third Breakthrough Communication Tool: Powerful Conversations

Everything lives in conversations. Consumers buy branded products because they hear conversations about the particular brand. These conversations spread, passed on from person to person and group to group in a cascade effect that builds or destroys, depending upon the story. One powerful example of the phenomenon of communications is Starbucks. There aren't many people who haven't heard of Starbucks, and people are willing to pay a high premium for a cup of Starbucks coffee because of potent conversations about the taste and the experience of drinking it. The company has done a superior job branding the product, and centering the brand on experiences. People meet at Starbucks. Interviewers hire people at Starbucks. Lovers, friends, husbands, and wives sit in Starbucks and have conversations.

Relationships live in conversations. How can a relationship survive without conversation? Conversations are the most powerful way to communicate, and the conversations we have either build or destroy. Conversations seep into the culture of an organization. The employees in a company have conversations that can either empower teams or create barriers amongst the members.

What people do, say, and believe lives on and is perpetuated in the stories they create. These stories affect the relationships among functions and departments and the corporate culture as a whole. *Marketing doesn't listen to us. Sales has all the money and power. Management doesn't care what we think.* These are common stories and conversations perpetuated in corporations. Though generally untrue, these stories become gossip, and serve only as barriers to organizational growth.

We create the stories of our lives based on our experiences shaped by our own internal filters and beliefs about the world. A story is not simply a record or narrative of what happened. It is our *interpretation* of what happened. So while it may contain some of the facts, it also contains a lot of the meanings we ascribed at the time, and since, to what happened. As time passes, the meaning of the story gets bigger, and though the actual event might be forgotten, the story remains. In our work of transforming businesses, we find that many managers talk nostalgically about their last place of work, sending the message—if only subconsciously—that the former place of employment was better than this one. This story builds and perpetuates. As it does, it has a dramatic and negative impact on current relationships.

Sometimes stories or metaphors can permeate an entire organization, or even a nation. Some remember the "Cold War era" while many believe we now live in the "post–9/11 era." Metaphors are powerful communication devices because they communicate with our unconscious mind. Metaphors are all around us. Our first fairy tales were metaphors; our dreams are metaphors; many movies are metaphors; advertising is a metaphor. We "rise and shine" in the morning and are "dead on our feet" by nighttime. We may think of life as a "struggle," as an "adventure," or even as "a box of chocolates." Metaphors can be magical or they can be destructive.

Metaphors are so powerful that they can shape our realities—or rather our experience of reality. In the Vietnam War era, the "domino theory" was a metaphor that suggested continued American involvement in Vietnam was necessary because if American troops pulled out the entire region would fall in dominolike fashion to communism. This was a powerful sensory metaphor. As children, many of us have played with dominoes this way. We know the certainty that if the first domino is tipped, the rest will tumble. The image of countries doing the same is chilling. The metaphor acts on our unconscious mind, where everything connects and is connected. This story kept America and its allies in Southeast Asia for a very long time, but what people didn't look at was the reality of the geography, the history of the countries, and the people who lived in those countries. Communism hadn't taken hold, and wasn't likely to, but fear perpetuated the story. People believed in it, and they lived, fought, and died under the metaphor of the domino theory.

Stories and metaphors in business can be damaging or productive. Businesses commonly use war metaphors such as "attacking the competition" or "being on the front line" and "hitting the target." As these metaphors take hold, people in an organization start to believe them. Someone says he's "living in the rat race," and before long, he sees his life and career as a rat race instead of a valuable, passionate, and worthy endeavor. Metaphors and stories are contagious, but businesses can manage them by finding a much more powerful and positive metaphor for the organization and defining it for people.

A Breakthrough Principle is that you need to manage your conversations—about your business, about your organization, about your brands—rather than having the conversations manage you.

The key distinction is to understand that a committed conversation is not just about something—it is directed toward a specific outcome. Conversations are not incidental. They shape the present moment and they shape our future. Conversations can keep us trapped in our histories or they can create openings into the future. Muhammad Ali kept up a conversation about himself from the days when he first started to fight. The conversation was, "I am the greatest." At first, he was the only one involved in that conversation and he provoked many to disagree. He's been quoted as saying, "When I first started saying 'I'm the Greatest,' even I didn't believe me." However, Ali continued to live in and live out this conversation until it eventually became reality.

So many of our daily conversations are *about* something—about something we have seen or heard, about something we are looking forward to, about something we are unhappy with, about something that has happened. For a conversation to really make a difference, though, it should intentionally generate an outcome.

For example, the key to building great ideas is to have many conversations for possibilities that will generate new possibilities and ideas. Framing it this way focuses the conversation on this outcome and minimizes the effects of Resigned Thinking. In this type of conversation, we will listen for possibilities and new ideas. A conversation that focuses on why the idea will not work or whether we have the time or budget may be an important topic but it is unlikely to generate possibilities. Conversations of that sort close down the possibilities for a breakthrough.

The most important conversation to generate is the conversation for the future. This is how we start to create change. After this, ongoing conversations sustain the change. This is the

Breakthrough approach to conversations. On the other hand, the Business as Usual approach is to get stuck in a conversation loop where we have the same conversations repeatedly.

In a very real way, brands are simply conversations. A company often designs a story around its brand. Think about the most powerful brands and the stories and feelings associated with them. Companies that develop successful brands design powerful stories. For years, Marlboro designed a story of power, freedom, and masculinity around the visual of a lone cowboy. Other companies design stories around their products that make the consumer feel something the company wants them to feel—something that associates strong and powerful emotions, images, and metaphors with their brand.

The Fourth Breakthrough Communication Tool: Background Conversations

Human beings have filters that affect the way we look at the world. A particular filter that largely affects our communications is what we call the Background Filter. This is the filter we carry about other people, situations, and projects. It contains thoughts, opinions, judgments, and ideas that we would not openly share.

We are often unaware of our Background Filter, and, like an invisible weight or burden, it has the effect of unconsciously affecting our energy, our communication, and our relationships with people. Like a camera filter, it often distorts our perceptions and judgments about others and ourselves.

Most conversations seem simple on the surface. However, there is more than meets the eye—or rather the ear. This is what it really looks like when two people are engaged in a conversation.

We call the conversation that is actually taking place between the two people the outer or foreground conversation. While this outer conversation is happening, each individual is also having another conversation in his head. This inner dialogue is

Conversations

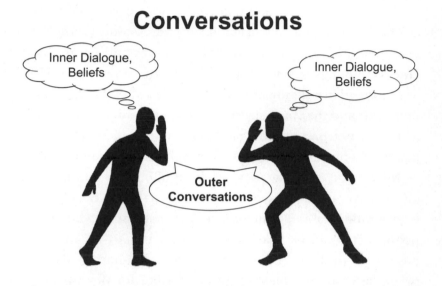

the Background Conversation, influenced by each individual's beliefs, values, opinions, and prejudices.

Becoming aware of this information and recognizing the filters we use will help us understand the way we interact with others. Once we have done this, we can identify whether our background belief about a person or group is accurate or a distortion—and can teach us why we have difficulties with particular people, departments, or organizations.

In work situations, Background Filters operate in virtually every interaction between individuals, teams, functions, and departments. The Background Filters we carry are often inaccurate, obsolete, or irrelevant. They create distortion and overgeneralizations in our perceptions and interpretations of others. When this happens, it can have a considerable negative impact upon our relationships and interactions with others. It is very empowering to become aware of the existence of these filters so we can have more choices in managing them. The key is keeping background information about others and situations as current, accurate, and relevant as possible.

For example, Bart's father was in the British army and fought against the Japanese in Burma during the Second World War. Even now, after sixty years, he still carries around Background Filters about Japan that he developed all those years ago. They were formed in a significant part of his life (when he was twenty years old) and they have stayed in the background, unchanged. Although not prejudiced against Japanese, he cannot look at Japan without seeing the country through his Background Filters.

In addition to being aware of these filters and letting them go whenever possible, we can choose to share our Background Conversations about someone or another group with those people. This can be risky. If not done skillfully, it can create even more problems than we had before, by sharing inappropriate thoughts and feelings that we harbor for the other person and not being able to resolve the resulting emotional reactions to our disclosure. But when used wisely and done skillfully (we recommend this exercise with the help of a skilled facilitator), it increases trust among individuals or groups. It is a way of opening the lines of communication. A general Breakthrough principle to remember is that the more Background Conversations there are between individuals or groups, the fewer possibilities there are for open, honest and effective communication.

Bart has a fascinating story that illustrates the value of uncovering Background Filters.

One day I was scheduled to meet with an American branch of a multinational pharmaceutical corporation then known as Ciba Geigy. The headquarters was in Switzerland and the Swiss CEO (who we were working with) suggested I meet with the American president. When I called to set up the appointment, he told me he didn't have time to meet with me. I said that I would be in the States for the entire week and was willing to meet him at any time at his convenience. He finally conceded to see me at 7 A.M. on Monday in New Jersey.

On Sunday, when I flew out from London, I realized that I had left my business suit on the back of my chair at home. I'd be arriving too late to find an open store, so I phoned Oscar, a friend of mine who lived in the States from the air phone, and asked if he had any suggestions about finding a suit. Oscar told me not to worry; we wore about the same size and he could messenger one of his suits to my hotel. At 2 A.M., I received a knock on the door. I opened the box from my friend, and inside I found a black suit with a short cut, Mexican bolero jacket—a bullfighter's suit. Oscar had quite a sense of humor.

In the morning, I made the best of things, put on the bullfighter's suit, and convinced myself it wouldn't look so bad. I had long hair those days so I slicked it back and tied it into a ponytail. I arrived at the company promptly at 7:00, but the president wasn't there and neither was anyone else, since most companies don't open their doors until eight. I waited, and as time passed, a few people arrived, walked right past me, and huddled in a group by the water cooler and coffeemaker. When the president walked in, I introduced myself and I asked how much time we would have for our discussion.

"I'll give you half an hour to show us what you're peddling," he said. "Then you're outta here!"

Remember, his CEO had recommended me. This was not a cold call. I knew by his response that I was in for trouble.

My first thought was that my dress sense must have offended him. My background at the time, coming from Europe, was that corporate America was very conservative as far as business dress was concerned. One just didn't show up to meetings in a bullfighting suit.

When the meeting began, I asked the president and everyone else in the room what they wanted to get out of the meeting. I began to use the Feedback Frame to elicit feedback, but the president interrupted me, pounded his fist on the desk, and said, "Look here; don't give us any of your psychogames! We're not going to stand for it."

His anger was intense, which was a big red flag that it didn't have anything to do with my suit or me. He was already on the Red Train, and I realized this president must have had some Background and Limiting Beliefs. I walked over to a big white board in the room and wrote down the word Consultant.

"What comes to mind when you think of this word?" I asked.

"Crook, charlatan, scoundrel," the president fired off immediately. "Ask 'em the time, they'll take your watch to tell you, break it, and then give it back to you."

As it turned out, the president had brought in one of the Big Five consulting firms for a high-profile project. The firm charged a large fee, promised a lot of solutions, and then never delivered. The president bore the brunt of it. He'd had a bad experience, and carried it with him as Background, projecting it onto Breakthrough.

"Well, I'm not a consultant," I told him. "Do I look like a consultant to you?" I figured this was a safe question since I knew of no consultants who wore bullfighting costumes.

"No," he said, "I guess not."

"I'm a coach. A consultant brings you the answers, but a coach helps you learn how to find them yourself. Have you had any experience with coaching?"

"Yes," he replied, and he told me how he had been the coach of his son's rugby team.

"When you coach the team, do you offer them answers?"

"No, not exactly. I help them develop the skills they need to improve themselves."

"Well, that's exactly what I do."

The tone of the meeting changed after this. The conversation became warmer and productive. My approach helped him get over his Backgrounds about consultants. We spent two hours together that day, and we implemented Breakthrough successfully within his organization after that.

The key to success was understanding that he was bringing Background into our meeting that had nothing to do with me and everything to do with his history. From this place, I was able to stay aware and uncover some of his Backgrounds and Limiting Beliefs. If he hadn't given me his open and honest feedback about consultants, I would have been spinning my wheels, trying to sell him something that I couldn't have paid him to take because he hated consultants that much.

The Fifth Breakthrough Communication Tool: Gossiping Success

Gossip will undermine the spirit of a team or organization with deadly efficiency—at least when that gossip is about gossiping failure. Within organizations, people gossip everywhere—in the corridors, by the coffee machine, in the bathrooms, etc. Unfortunately, gossip tends to focus on negatives and this has a massive impact on energy, morale, and empowerment.

Four main conversations typify gossiping failure. The first is the complaint. This conversation feeds itself and exists everywhere in business culture and in much of life outside. Complaining comes from a worldview of scarcity. In the world of scarcity, there is never enough—time, money, people, resources, trust, reward, recognition, etc. Interestingly, in this world of scarcity, there is also too much—bureaucracy, control, time wasting, work, travel, and so on. The complainer is very rarely fully committed to resolving his complaint. He's just trying to hook the listener into his story. Being hooked requires little more than a nod of the head. The most effective way to deal with the complainer is to ask the question, "What do you intend to do about it?"

The second conversation is very similar and comes in two forms—the Victim story and the Martyr story. The victim story sends the message, "It's not my fault, but . . ." Other people—usually "they"—are the cause of the victim's suffering. These stories tend to leave out relevant information that makes the speaker seem less like a victim. The martyr story is essentially the same, with the addition of "And they just don't appreciate how much I've sacrificed . . ."

The third gossiping conversation is the blame story. The primary message of this story is, "It's all your fault." In this conversation, the recipient of the conversation becomes the cause of all of the things that are not going right. The speaker makes harsh judgments and often labels people in abusive ways.

The fourth gossiping conversation is the learned helplessness story. In this conversation, the speaker is disempowered. "I've tried everything; there's nothing else I can do." "It's no use giving my boss my feedback—it wouldn't change anything if I did."

One thing common to these four stories is that by living in these conversations, the speaker does not have to take responsibility for the situation he is in or for doing something about it. For many people, this is the easy option. For many it is also an unconscious choice.

The answer to this is not trying to *stop* gossiping. Telling groups of people not to gossip is tantamount to telling them not to breathe. Gossiping is a natural human activity. However, by encouraging a different kind of gossip—Gossiping Success—the results are decidedly different.

Gossiping Success is not about putting a positive spin on things. Gossiping Success is about the power of language and how it affects perspective and emotion. It is about being very honest about what has happened and recognizing both the positives and the negatives. Gossiping Success simply means making an intentional effort to focus on the positive, and to recognize and stop the unproductive habit of gossiping negativity. Imagine the environment and energy in an organization that recognizes and gossips about the successes of team members and the company.

One of Bart's clients, Anika, was the CFO of a large global business. During our sessions, he quickly noticed that whenever she described her situation or Bart made a suggestion to her, she would always start her answer with, "You see, the problem is . . ." and then tell him about the barriers in her way. When Bart recognized this pattern, he brought it to her attention. She had no idea she did this *at all,* let alone repeatedly.

Understanding that Anika's behavior was unconscious, Bart realized he would have to use shock tactics to break this pattern. The next time she started with the phrase "You see the problem is," he jumped up onto his chair and squealed, "Yeooow!"

This worked. Anika was shocked and stopped in midsentence. "What's wrong?" she asked.

"You said, 'The problem is,' but there is no problem," Bart said.

She looked suspicious. "Did I really say that?"

The next time she said the phrase, Bart again jumped up to stand on his chair and gave a loud squeal. This time Anika said, "Did I say it again?" This went on until Anika picked up on the pattern. Eventually she stopped saying it. Bart's shock tactics changed her awareness and through that, she broke her pattern. This went beyond language, though. As her language changed, she stopped living in the conversation that everything was a problem. She became visibly lighter and more energized.

Conversations for Gossiping Success are empowering and energizing. They do not come from the complainer, victim, blamer, or holder of helpless mind-sets. Instead, they come from an appreciative mind-set—discovering the many things that we can be appreciative about within a person, a team, a project, or an organization. One definition of "appreciate" is "to create value" (as in, when our investments appreciate). Gossiping Success serves the same function. Gossiping Success builds relationships and is a key building block of building great teams. Remember that words create worlds and that positive conversations create positive change.

A Breakthrough principle is that in a business, at every minute during the day you are either *Adding Cost* or *Adding Value*. Time and energy spent milling about in the corridors, complaining about other people, adds cost. We all gossip, yet Gossiping Success can acknowledge people; it can empower them toward accomplishments, motivate them, and inspire them. This kind of gossip adds value. We encourage our clients to Gossip Success as often as they can. We encourage them to institutionalize this Breakthrough tool by Gossiping Success at the start of every meeting. Duke Petrovich, chief administrative officer at the Wrigley Company, has become a master of this throughout the organization. Not only is he quick to acknowl-edge success he sees on his travels around the company, but he also passes along stories of others from throughout the organi-zation. He recognizes people's contributions immediately and publicly, and he chooses to share success stories that inspire and empower people within and outside his functional area.

Changing an entire organization or culture seems difficult when we think of this as changing people, structures, and pro-cesses. However, if we only have to change the conversation, the mission seems easier. Conversations can change with only a thought or a word. As we saw with Anika, changing someone's language changes the person. True transformation starts by changing the conversation. As more and more people are en-rolled into the new conversation about the future, the organiza-tion starts to change.

What Breakthrough Communicators Know

Breakthrough Communicators have a distinct advantage over those with lesser communication skills because they can use their abilities to build their people and establish stronger rela-tionships. Breakthrough Communicators understand the per-suasive power of listening and providing powerful feedback. They intentionally manage their conversations and understand the impact these conversations have on an organization's cul-ture and climate. They realize how much can be gained from seeing things from another's point of view.

They know that words have extraordinary power and that powerful words can drive a team to new heights.

Putting Breakthrough Communications to Work

You can create an environment within your organization where communication becomes an invaluable tool for growth. Start by changing the way you and your team listen. Learn to shape the listening environment of your workplace to enable people to be more expressive and creative in their communication and to hear feedback in a nondefensive way. Again, start with yourself. At your next meeting, make an active effort to listen more carefully to what is being said. Notice when your inner voice interrupts. Rather than convincing yourself that you know what the speaker is going to say or that you need to prepare your response, shut the door on your inner voice instead. Concentrate on the speaker. You'll have time to formulate a response later if necessary.

Now observe how others on your team are listening. Can you tell when their inner voices cut in? What conversations are they having with that voice? What is the impact on the meeting? When you become adept at silencing your inner voice, share this skill with your team. Acknowledge that the inner voice is always present, but show that it is possible to turn the volume down.

Next, make the Feedback Frame a standard working tool in your organization. Use the frame to shape all discussions where feedback is necessary—everything from performance reviews to progress reports to rehearsals for presentations to meeting follow-up. Walk your team through the four quadrants of the frame; make sure they understand the purpose of each quadrant and that they can use each to give and receive constructive, nondefensive feedback. When used correctly, the Feedback Frame is a hugely beneficial tool. If every member of your team employs it, communications within your company will improve exponentially. Have team members pair up and practice giving feedback to one another using the frame. It won't take long before they gain expertise and make it a natural part of their communications.

As they develop expertise in the Feedback Frame, you can teach your team about Background Conversations. As with so many of these tools, it is important for you to understand how this affects you before you can help others with it. Teach yourself to become more aware of the Background Filters you carry about others. It helps in this case to write things down. Write what you "know" about your team, people in other functions, your customers, your competitors, and the marketplace. When you write these things, reach for the items you find difficult to acknowledge or that you would never say to the person in question. These very items—fears, prejudices, limiting beliefs, etc.—are the things that sit in the background and have a debilitating impact on your relationships. Writing them down brings them to the surface, shows you how they might have a dampening effect on growth, and allows you to deal with them.

Now have your team do the same thing. Make it clear that they are doing this in a safe environment and that honesty won't have negative consequences. Once they've made their lists, facilitate a discussion about their findings. Encourage them to create strategies for dealing with what they've uncovered. Help them to understand that Background Filters are usually generalized stereotypes, that stereotypes are often too broad to have meaning with any individual, and that these stereotypes hinder relationships and communications.

Finally, teach your team how to Gossip Success. Remember, we all have a natural tendency to gossip. When we gossip about negative things, it hurts the organization. However, if we gossip about our achievements, the organization is energized. Make a list of your company's recent accomplishments. Be intentional about finding a way to gossip another item on this list every day. Start every meeting by going around the room to allow each team member to talk about recent successes. Create a "success forum," a tool the organization can utilize to spread the word about what they've done together. This can be an e-mail discussion group or a forum on the company's intranet. It can be an electronic or paper newsletter. It can be a bulletin board. The goal is to create a place where team members can participate regularly and view the participations of others.

Doing all of this in an intentional way will change the nature of communication on your team. This, in turn, will engage, enlighten, and inspire all involved.

CHAPTER SEVEN

FULL-ON

Founded in Flint, Michigan, near the turn of the twentieth century, in 1955 General Motors became the first American corporation to make more than one billion dollars in a year. The company was on top of the world. A couple of years earlier, Charles Erwin Wilson, then GM president, became the secretary of defense of the United States. When asked if he could make a decision in his new position adverse to the interests of GM, he responded that he couldn't conceive such a situation because, "I thought what was good for the country was good for General Motors and vice versa." At the time, General Motors was one of the largest employers in the world and an enormous force in American business.

Decades hence, however, General Motors had slipped from its lofty perch. A particularly poignant illustration of this arose when Ross Perot sold his company, an entrepreneurial, high-energy organization called EDS, to GM for two and a half billion dollars in 1984. With the sale, Perot secured a position on GM's board of directors. Perot thought he could change the culture of GM, but he found it to be almost impossible. "Revitalizing General Motors is like teaching an elephant to dance," he said. "You find the sensitive spots and start poking." It turned out that the elephant was too big and Perot could not find enough sensitive spots. He tried to get GM management to face its problems, but they ran in the other direction. Frustrated and disappointed, Perot departed four years later with a hefty severance package and started a new data processing company, Perot Systems Corp.

Once a landmark profit maker, GM posted a loss of four and a half billion dollars in 1992. In response, the board demoted the company's president, Lloyd Reuss, and removed chairman Robert Stempel from the board's executive committee. Unfortunately, neither move did much to reverse the corporation's fortunes.

How did this happen?

In the 1950s, GM innovated. It built convenience into its cars, made them larger, and added distinctive decorative features such as tail fins. GM led the transformation from manual to automatic transmissions, making cars easier for customers to drive. It built high-compression engines, increasing horsepower and speed. It strove to understand the needs of American drivers and to exceed those needs.

As the company became bigger and started making a lot of money, though, its people became complacent and energy waned. GM stood by and watched as the competition grew stronger. The company believed that American consumers would always buy American out of a sense of patriotism. They didn't think they needed to try as hard as the foreign car manufacturers seeking to enter the market. Meanwhile, Volkswagen broke ground with its Beetle, and Toyota and Nissan took baby steps into America. As time passed, these imported cars continued to learn from consumer experiences and made improvements. GM only continued to fail to respond. When gas prices soared in the seventies, sales of foreign cars rose accordingly while GM found itself unable to launch small models. GM had lost the energy and intentionality necessary to innovate. It took them five years to change a model while foreign competitors exhibited extraordinary flexibility.

Despite massive investments in new plants and technology, GM failed to build the culture of innovation in its people. In the 1980s, GM needed four and a half people to build one car per day as compared to less than three for foreign competitors. These labor costs have continued to rise. In 2005, it was estimated that GM's employee health costs added sixteen hundred dollars to the price of each car compared with less than two hundred dollars per car for Toyota. In response to its flagging performance, GM has undergone various cost-reduction strategies rather than building an innovative high-energy culture. This has led to morale problems, a further reduction in employee energy, and a lack of the commitment so essential for the long-term success of any company.

In the beginning of 2006, GM announced losses of 10.6 billion dollars. It was once the model of the powerful American corporation, a symbol of the American dream.

Now it is a symbol of a condition we call "Full-Off."

Mead Johnson Nutritionals, a subsidiary of Bristol Myers Squibb, had been a pioneer in the development of nutritional infant formula with their brand Emfamil. The company's founder, Edward (Mead) Johnson, developed this formula to save his newborn son, who could not digest mother's milk. Mr. Johnson knew his newborn son was not alone in his condition and wanted to provide this nutritional alternative to mother's milk to save those infants as well. He launched his company in the small midwestern town of Evansville, Indiana, and started selling the formula to doctors. By the late 1980s, Mead Johnson Nutritionals had developed into a multibillion-dollar business.

The entrepreneurial spirit combined with strong work ethics and midwestern values helped Mead Johnson rise as a strong growth business until Bristol Myers Squibb acquired the company in the early nineties. Bristol installed its own management from the East Coast, stripped Mead Johnson of some of its emerging businesses, and laid off many employees.

In the process, it stripped away the entrepreneurial spirit of the organization. The focus of the executive team shifted from innovation to career enhancement. Leadership understood that most of the business decisions were being made in Bristol's headquarters in New York and strove to be relocated there. Mead Johnson went from being an aggressive creator of new products to a cash cow for the development of prescription drugs in Bristol.

Surinder joined Mead Johnson as senior vice president of R&D in 1998. The company was in a seemingly constant state of transition, having recently fired its president, Ian Stuart, after he'd been in the position for less than two years. Employees were so accustomed to changes in management that they barely reacted. Surinder attempted to bring Breakthrough thinking and a new sense of energy to the company, but he soon realized that the Mead Johnson staff had made the collective decision to invest less of themselves in the company. He noted very healthy attitudes among the staff regarding their home lives, but little passion about work.

Little has changed at Mead Johnson in the ensuing years. The company is not in desperate straits (as GM is), but it lacks any cogent business strategy. It expanded product development from infant formula to nutritional products for toddlers, women, and geriatrics, and then made the decision to sell both its adult medical and women's nutritional businesses. With this lack of strategy comes a lack of identity. There is no clear sense of Mead Johnson's mission and this is reflected in the energy and commitment levels of its people. The employees feel they have no control over their destinies. They feel no sense of ownership.

Mead Johnson sits in an uncomfortable middle space that we call "Guess-So."

In the late seventies and early eighties when Pizza Hut was growing at a record pace, their success attracted the attention of competitors such as Domino's, Little Caesar's, and other regional and national pizza chains. Steve Reinemund had just become the president of the company, focusing Pizza Hut on developing great-tasting products, building sit-down restaurants across the United States, and expanding globally. This strategy was consistent with the company's record of success, but it failed to accommodate a revolution happening under their noses. While Pizza Hut continued to build expensive restaurants, Domino's developed the insight that Americans actually seemed to prefer to enjoy pizza in the comfort of their own homes.

Domino's began building the distribution network and logistics for delivering pizza to consumers' homes with guaranteed delivery within thirty minutes of the order. The strategy was wildly successful, and before long Domino's had a strong share of the pizza business without wasting money on expensive restaurants. As Domino's sales soared, those at Pizza Hut stagnated.

At the time, Pizza Hut was a division of PepsiCo. Throughout the corporation's hallways, executives speculated and second-guessed about the declining fortunes of the restaurant chain. Dire scenarios emerged. When PepsiCo held its next biannual meeting in Whistler, Canada, most Pizza Hut employees were nervous. The goal of each biannual meeting was to review every business, align key executives on the vision, and plan for the future—and the future seemed unknowable for Pizza Hut.

At the meeting, Steve Reinemund walked to the podium to address his division's condition. "In the past," he said, "we were focused on building from our current business model. However, we missed a beat on the emerging business model necessary to deliver on what consumers want now. I promise you that we will learn from this and Pizza Hut will emerge as a stronger innovator and leader."

Reinemund restated the direction in which the company would go. He didn't make excuses for the past, and he communicated confidence to the team with powerful language. He knew he needed to overcome the uncertainty. He knew that he needed to enroll the top management of PepsiCo and energize the Pizza Hut team. From this point forward, Reinemund created an inspired and intentional organization committed to winning. As a result, Pizza Hut quickly and successfully entered the pizza delivery business and relegated Domino's to a second-tier company. The spirit of energy, intentionality, and focus that drove Pizza Hut out of its difficult phase continued as the company expanded its business into the Soviet Union, Korea, Eastern Europe, China, and India.

This combination of energy, intentionality, and focus is a condition we call "Full-On."

The Function of Energy

Energy is the difference between life and death, the power that moves the world, and the resource that makes everything happen. At various times, a person experiences high levels of energy and when low, summons an increase in energy or finds such an increase impossible. Our bodies control energy through a process known as thermoregulation. Through this process, nutrients are converted into energy and released as heat. This is largely unconscious and involuntary, but it is possible for a person—through awareness of the body's energy thermostat—to have greater control over the intensity of his energy level.

Energy thermostats control internal physiological, mental, or emotional energy states. Imagine an old-fashioned power lever, like the ones at the helm of a boat. When the lever is near the off position, the boat has little power and doesn't go very far. A person whose lever is near the off position is at extremely low energy and, like the boat, won't get very far. In the Full-On

Full-Off ➜ Full-On

Full-Off   Guess-So   Full-On

position, however, the boat is charged with energy and cuts briskly through the water. A person whose energy thermostat lever is in the Full-On position is fully alive, accomplishing tasks at a surprising—even unimaginable—rate. We all can think of a time when our energy lever was in the Full-On position, when our physiological, mental, and emotional energy were all in the same place at the same time. When the body, mind, and emotions are all in the same place at the same time, one is "in the moment."

Most people do not live this way very often. Instead, most people live with their emotions in the past (feelings of guilt and resentment) and their minds in the future (fears or concerns about outcomes that may or may not ever happen). Such a disconnect makes it nearly impossible to be Full-On. Children, however, spend a significant amount of time in Full-On mode. Four- or five-year-olds do whatever they are doing—playing, eating, watching a movie, even sleeping—with complete commitment.

Most people are living with their energy thermostats at the middle position, about halfway between Full-Off and Full-On. We refer to this as the "Guess-So" state. *Are you glad to be here?* "Guess so." *Would you like to take on this challenging assignment?* "Guess so." The middle position is one of noncommittal indifference and nondirected energy. The boat goes, but not particularly fast and not in any specific direction.

Like individuals, companies operate within these three energy states. Pizza Hut became a Full-On company when it made the decision to surpass Domino's in the pizza delivery business— and has maintained that sense of energy even though they accomplished the task. The energy at Mead Johnson is far less intense. The staff doesn't know where the company is going and therefore can't make a determined effort to get there. The energy level at GM is barely discernable. The company isn't moving forward at all and one could argue that it is rapidly moving backward.

Energy states have a tremendous impact on the results an organization can achieve. When energy is high, the results are greater. When it's low, the potential output and productivity decreases. Energy is vital to success and it can affect the feeling and productivity of a business culture. Identifying a company's energy state and shifting it, if necessary, to Full-On is critical to putting that company on a Breakthrough trajectory.

The Full-Off Organization

As we saw with the GM example, the Full-Off company operates from a position of depleted energy. The reasons for this sense of depletion can be numerous—abusive management, onerous expectations, adverse market conditions, seemingly invincible competition, etc.—but the upshot is an organization that is going nowhere.

Realistically, "going nowhere" is an overly generous appraisal. When GM loses more than ten billion dollars in a single year, it isn't simply "going nowhere"—it is rapidly going backward. It is heading toward oblivion. The overwhelming risk of a Full-Off organization is that continuing in this state for any length of time might put the organization out of existence.

Some companies have an atmosphere of drained energy that you can literally feel when you enter the building. The physical environment is an obvious clue—drab walls, gray cubicles, low lighting. This low-energy environment depletes the energy of the people within the organization and when the energy of the people is depleted, the organization is in real trouble.

Curiously, while an outsider can see these palpable signs of energy loss, people within a Full-Off organization rarely can. It's a bit like living in a house for a long time and losing the ability to see where it needs repairs. These companies need an energy intervention. They have not realized how vital energy is to a workforce and how it affects results. Energy at the individual level affects the entire culture. The energy of the organization affects the individual. Energy is a thread that weaves through the organization connecting people, teams, and departments. It travels horizontally and vertically and has the power to sustain, build, offer momentum, or destroy. Positive inspirational energy can drive people to achieve phenomenal results. An atmosphere of negative or depleted energy is likely to have the opposite effect.

Full-Off organizations are in a crisis state. Failure to "turn on the engines" leads to an untimely end. Think of a person with absolutely no energy. We have another word for that: dead. Full-Off organizations are close to death.

The only way for GM to escape this fate is to suffuse the entire organization with energy, intentionality, and focus. This will not be easy after decades of inertia, but it is essential if this great American company is to have a future in the new century. We'll talk more about how companies make this shift at the end of this chapter.

The Guess-So Organization

Most organizations operate in Guess-So mode most of the time. Guess-So companies tend to focus on process rather than inspiration. They become caught up in the details of running an operation, focusing on tried-and-true methods rather than breaking new ground. Guess-So organizations rely on business as usual thinking rather than the kind of magical thinking that leads to Breakthrough.

Energy levels in Guess-So organizations are lower than they could be because the leaders of those organizations want to minimize risk. They believe that taking aggressive chances will lead to costly errors. The reality, though, is that *not* taking risks *increases* the odds of failure. While more aggressive, Full-On competitors redefine the market and gain greater share, the Guess-So organization plods ahead with tired models. The result might not be as disastrous as a high-risk blunder, but the slow erosion of market share is nearly guaranteed.

Companies switch into this mode when a change causes the people within an organization to feel that they've lost control of their destinies. Remember what happened at Mead Johnson? This innovative, Full-On company slipped into Guess-So mode because new ownership stripped the organization of its sense of mission. When it became clear to the people in Evansville, Indiana, that the people in New York were calling all the shots, energy levels took a tumble. The Mead Johnson staff lost its sense of "ownership." In its place came a sense of disempowerment, which made it nearly impossible to stay Full-On. Afraid and confused, the people within that organization chose to concentrate their energies on home and give less than their best at work. Even the introduction of Breakthrough techniques couldn't help because the management at Bristol Meyers Squibb failed to change the environment.

The Full-On Organization

The energy level of a Full-On organization is palpable. It is visible in the company's meeting rooms and corridors, in their advertising campaigns, and even in the artwork on the walls of their offices. The Full-On organization is dedicated to applying all of its resources all of the time. Leaders of Full-On organizations understand that true growth only comes when innovation is constant. Steve Reinemund understood that business as usual would have been disastrous at Pizza Hut. He inspired his people with a mission—to reinvent the company in the face of new market challenges—and provided them with the tools necessary to stay energized and intentional. The effect of this inspiration was so strong that the company stayed in this mode long after they'd conquered the pizza delivery business and reestablished their primacy. This led to even greater innovation and the Full-On entry into new global markets.

Virtually all organizations are in Full-On mode at start-up. Realistically, any start-up that operates at Full-Off or Guess-So levels will not stay in business very long. Start-ups need to create a place for themselves in the market. They need to establish their competitive edge. They strive to be noticed and to find ways to stand out in the crowd. This requires a very high level of energy applied over an extended period.

True Full-On organizations find a way to maintain this spirit once they pass the start-up phase. They retain (or recapture if they've managed to slip into one of the other modes) a commitment to innovation and invention, knowing that they can only truly succeed if they keep growing. Full-On organizations aren't afraid of risks, even when those risks could lead to big failures. What Full-On companies realize is that the full deployment of the energies of its people will generate more than enough achievement to overcome any misstep.

When a person is Full-On, he speaks clearly and with conviction (think of the intentional way Steve Reinemund announced his company's new objectives). He's fully engaged in life. He looks you straight in the eye, and when he speaks, others listen. He encourages others by his example to quickly identify business opportunities and respond to change with enthusiasm. He is fully alive. An entire organization filled with these people creates extraordinary things.

Building Energy

Great leaders are able to maximize the potential of diverse members of their teams. In the science of physical chemistry, there is a concept known as "activation energy." This describes the energy required to cause a chemical reaction between two substances. In effect, when the two substances react, they can create products that have higher chemical energy than the combined energy of the individual substances. Alternatively, a catalyst can be used to cause the reaction between the two substances, leading to a higher energy product.

The same concept applies to people. When individuals interact, they may create a team that has higher level of energy than the combined energy of the individuals. Breakthrough leaders provide that "activation energy" or act as the catalysts to cause such interaction amongst their people. These are Breakthrough teams working with higher power and velocity to achieve extraordinary outcomes. Transformation from Guess-So or Full-Off company to Full-On company calls for leaders who are capable of providing activation energy and catalyzing change.

James Cash Penney, the founder of JC Penney, once said, "In every man's life there lies latent energy. There is, however, a spark, that if kindled, will set the whole being afire, and he will become a human dynamo, capable of accomplishing almost anything to which he aspires." Every individual has two types of energy, potential and kinetic. Potential energy is the total energy one has available. Kinetic energy is the energy one puts to work for oneself. When a person is sitting at his desk or in a meeting, most of his energy is being stored as potential energy. Nothing much gets accomplished when the energy form is only in this phase. If a fire alarm went off in that meeting, though, potential energy would quickly become kinetic energy. Kinetic energy creates momentum. It moves things, and produces results.

When we take Breakthrough into an organization, we teach leaders and managers how to keep their people in Full-On mode, to remain in the energy zone with the greatest opportunity for accelerated success. A great leader excels at increasing the energy within his organization. He continually builds the people, therefore building the business, and finds ways to tap into the latent energy sources that will facilitate personal and professional growth.

In the Breakthrough program, we ask participants to map out where they believe their company is on the energy thermostat. We create a diagram with the three modes and then ask them to think of a Full-On company, whether it's their own or another, and to write the name of that company on the thermostat diagram. Inevitably, companies like Google or Southwest Airlines show up as Full-On companies. We continue this process through the other two modes. The companies that always seem to show up in the Guess-So zone tend to be companies perceived as stodgy and bureaucratic, companies that do business as usual. Companies in the Full-Off zone tend to be those in serious and very public trouble.

We then ask participants to put their own companies on the diagram, along with their direct competitors. This is often highly instructive, especially when the participants list their own company as Guess-So and their leading competitor as Full-On. This exercise often leads to intensive discussions about building energy.

Energy shifts are all about leadership. We feel very strongly that companies can only transform if the leader chooses to start with himself. This means personifying Full-On behaviors and energy. The leader who simply talks about changing the energy of an organization is missing the point. Again, let's go back to Steve Reinemund. When he realized that he needed to move Pizza Hut out of its Guess-So state, he concurrently realized that he had to recharge himself. He set high, inspiring goals and presented it to his staff as a rallying cry. He spoke with energy, intentionality, and focus. If he'd simply identified the problem without addressing the solution energetically his efforts would have failed.

Once the leader leads the charge toward Full-On, he needs

to focus on outcomes. This is about keeping an eye on those ambitious goals. The energy of an organization stays high when it is reminded constantly that it has something bold to achieve. Hand in hand with this is the encouragement of experimentation. Growth requires risk and Full-On companies reward risk-takers and refrain from punishing setbacks. These companies understand that the path to success is rarely a straight line and the occasional "failure" is part of the process. At the same time, every person needs to feel accountable (more on this later in the book) and those who achieve results and exhibit Full-On behavior must be rewarded.

Most important, organizations seeking to shift from Full-Off or Guess-So to Full-On need to be sure to enroll their employees in this future vision. It is impossible to have a Full-On organization if the staff lacks a clear idea of the company's mission. In order to kick an organization into Full-On mode, buy-in is required at every level; the entire team needs to embrace the value of change in achieving the new vision. When it does, profound energy shifts occur.

The Four Energy States

In our work, we have identified four distinct energy states. They are low positive, high positive, low negative, and high negative. Each energy state affects the trajectory of an organization. The best leaders we've worked with understand energy states and pay attention to them, working to monitor their organization's state constantly.

People spend much of their most productive time in a low positive energy state, in activities such as reading or conducting research. Low positive energy is critical for sustaining energy, because it utilizes passive activity. As such, it is an essential component of being Full-On. When a person is reading, thinking, or even meditating, he is in a low positive energy state yet still gaining knowledge and recharging his batteries. Traits of a low positive energy state include reflection, serenity, and a sense of relaxation. When this state permeates an organization, the organization can move smoothly toward challenges.

High positive is an exciting energy state. In it, one can create and accelerate, but this energy state can be difficult to maintain over extended periods. In this high-energy mode, people tend to be exhausted by the end of the day with little energy left over for family, relationships, or anything else. People and organizations successfully in Full-On mode, therefore, strike a balance between low positive and high positive states. Traits of a high positive energy state include enthusiasm, euphoria, passion, and excitement. When an organization is charged with high positive energy, it invites challenges and overcomes hurdles with ease.

In a low negative energy state, negative energy affects performance at work and in everyday activities. Performance and self-confidence fall to dangerous levels, and someone operating in this state for a persistent period might appear to be going with the flow, when they have actually simply checked out. Traits of a low negative energy state include apathy, depression, and burnout. Low negative energy is common in Guess-So organizations and is an indicator of decline toward Full-Off.

High negative is a particularly destructive state. In this mode, a person or an organization has a high amount of negative energy that fuels every thought, feeling, and action. People in a high negative energy state tend to drain energy from those around them. Traits of a high negative energy state are anger, frustration, pain, and cynicism. An organization filled with high negative energy is one at serious risk of becoming Full-Off.

Most people do not realize that the state they are in will influence the results of whatever they are doing. People unconsciously put a great deal of energy and effort into trying to control the environment and other people when, in fact, the only control anyone has is over himself. Controlling one's own energy state not only has an impact on the results one gets, but also determines the quality of life one experiences and one's output in the workplace.

Breakthrough leaders help others understand their states and help them move toward more positive states if necessary. This often happens when a management change brings a Full-On leader on board. When Lee Iacocca took over Chrysler, he diagnosed a lack of innovation that was hindering a company once built on innovation. To remedy this, he generated new ideas that spurred his people on with a new sense of energy. He introduced the seven-year warranty, challenging his people to build cars that lasted. He developed the K-cars, a new, highly innovative set of vehicles that pushed Chrysler back onto the Full-On track.

IBM was a Guess-So company under John Akers. He hired brilliant scientists and engineers, but he didn't link their work with business outcomes. The result was a lack of direction throughout the organization. The mission of the company was not clear. When Lou Gerstner replaced him, he brought with him a sense of business discipline and focus. He demanded that IBM achieve palpable business results. In doing so, he moved IBM back into Full-On mode. The entire organization knew their mission and set out to achieve it.

Mental, physical, and emotional energy are closely related, and each one affects the other. The words one uses as an individual creates, builds, or depletes energy within a team. Body language and thought processes also affect the overall energy of the team.

When we implement Breakthrough within a corporation, the first thing we do is open the session with bodywork—various stretching and breathing exercises designed to get the blood flow moving through their bodies and literally wake them up. For those who consider exercise running late for a meeting, it's a real revelation. Sometimes we get grumbles and rolling of the eyes, but by the second day everyone is engaged and they value the opportunity to get their bodies energized in new ways. For the employees who are used to working out and staying physically fit, the bodywork is an enhancement to the program and perhaps reaffirms their own internal principles about energy management.

Full-On is a Breakthrough principle that effectively predicts an organization's long-term chances of success. When an organization is Full-Off, it is likely to suffer dramatic losses. When an organization is Guess-So, it stands a very good chance of losing ground to the competition. However, when it is Full-On, its horizons are limitless. The competition stands very little chance of gaining on them because the staff is energized, focused, and moving forward with strong intentionality. Full-On organizations live in the Breakthrough zone of magical thinking and heroic actions. They think creatively and execute heroically with excellence to continue to build energy, passion, and their businesses. Full-On organizations are very difficult to beat, and believe they are invincible.

Putting Full-On to Work

Switching your organization's power lever to the Full-On position starts with engaging that lever in yourself. Full-On means that you are intentional, focused, and energized. We like to tell people that being Full-On means being "proactively proactive."

A journal is a good way to monitor your state and keep your energy level high. Keep a list of things, situations, and people that drain your energy. Be as honest with yourself as possible. Are there some surprises on this list? Once you have this list, commit it to memory, and minimize your encounters with these things, situations, and people. Anything that drains your energy puts you at risk of flipping over to Guess-So mode. Too much exposure can even turn you Full-Off.

Now create a list of things, situations, and people that help you generate energy. There will probably be fewer surprises on this list, but this list has at least as much value as the first list. Consider this your "go-to" list. Whenever you need an extra jolt of energy or feel your energy state slipping, get involved with the things, situations, and people you have on this second list. Focusing your time on maximizing exposure to the items on the second list and minimizing exposure to the items on the first list will drive you toward a consistent Full-On state.

Model this for your team. Explain the concepts of Full-On, Guess-So, and Full-Off and show them how only one of these states leads to meaningful growth. Set high expectations and outcomes for the team—outcomes that can only be reached if the team operates Full-On. Remain focused on these outcomes until the team achieves them and then immediately set new outcomes.

Be sure to celebrate every milestone your team reaches. By doing so, you reinforce the incredible power of Full-On energy.

CHAPTER EIGHT

LINE OF ONE

When Bart worked at Unilever early in his career, he attended an Outward Bound Leadership program in New Mexico. In this program, a hundred people were divided into teams of ten and these teams competed against each other over a week's time.

On the first night, Bart was chagrined to realize that he'd been assigned to a team of losers. That, of course, was not their official designation, but it was clear that they were the weakest physical specimens in the entire program—and the competitions were primarily physical. One competition was a military exercise with an obstacle course in which the team had to cross a river, climb over a thirty-foot cargo net, crawl through a fifty-yard sewer pipe, and even jump through flaming hoops. The second part of the competition was an archery event and the organizers kept the details about the third part a mystery. The obvious favorite among the ten teams was a team from Australia. All of their members were young, fit, and tanned. Bart was not encouraged by the outlook. The group's first assignment in the program was to create a team banner with fingerpaints. To Bart, this seemed like a simple kindergarten activity, a waste of time and money. The program's organizers told all participants that they had to do everything as a team. Once they were finished, each team needed to bring their banner, along with a rope and a twenty-foot tree trunk to a great tent up on the mountain at five o'clock the next morning. The tree trunk—which ultimately became part of the obstacle course—was a literal burden to the team. It was extremely heavy and the team had to carry it everywhere it went. At one point, they even had to drag it through the sewage pipe buried in the hillside.

It took about an hour to get to the tent, so that meant leaving at four A.M. The next morning, Bart set off alone and was the first to arrive at the tent. When he got there, the organizers asked him where the rest of his team was as well as the rope, trunk, and banner. Bart explained that the rest of the team was on its way as were (he assumed) the materials. As the rest of the team straggled in however, the rope, trunk, and banner were nowhere in sight. No one had assumed the leadership necessary to bring these things.

The training sessions were grueling and Bart's team returned exhausted every day from these exercises in the mountains and forest. They were always the last team to enter the camp and when they did, they were asked if they wanted to join a volleyball game. With no energy and less spirit, they declined and went to their separate rooms.

At the end of a long, tiring, and miserable week, the teams had their final practice session before the actual competition. Things did not look good for Bart's team. There was discontent and infighting everywhere, and some people simply refused to climb over the thirty-foot cargo net. This meant instant disqualification because each team member needed to complete the course. The stronger team members tried different tactics to get the weakest members of the team involved, including bullying, guilt-tripping, and pleading. They got nowhere with any of these approaches. The final run-through was a disaster and Bart anticipated extreme embarrassment during the competition the next day. His team looked and acted like losers.

The night before the competition, depressed about the group's prospects, Bart had a breakthrough. Since the team had no leader, he realized that he needed to step into the breach and serve that role. First, though, he would have to gain the team's acceptance and trust. He remembered once participating in the Native American Talking Stick ritual in which a sacred space was created in the form of a circle around a fire. In the circle, an intricately carved stick was passed from person to person like a peace pipe. As each participant took the stick, he went into the center of the circle and addressed the group while everyone else was quiet. Each speaker said something to acknowledge or honor someone in the group, to inspire or empower the group, or to share a story. At the end of each speaker's turn, the whole group responded with *"Homoi taqui essa"* (we are connected) or just *"Ho."*

Bart decided to use the Talking Stick ritual as a way to break the ice that had formed among members of his team and get them to the point where they would start to trust each other. It worked exactly as he hoped. As the Talking Stick went around, the doors of communication opened, creating a safe environment for expression. The team learned that the two or three people who refused to cross the cargo net did so because they were terrified. They didn't believe they could do it and were afraid of crashing down to the ground below. The effort required to overcome this fear was beyond the limits of their courage. Bart tried to find out what they needed in order to cross over, and they said they needed someone strong standing below the net to catch them in case they fell. In the practice exercises, the team had been sending the strongest climbers across first, so they could rush over to the river and start building the rope bridge that was the next part of the exercise. This turned out to be a huge mistake because, by doing this, the team left the ones who were afraid to climb alone.

The Talking Stick exercise changed the dynamics within the team. They'd aired differences and come to understand each other. Knowing that most of the other teams were superior physically, they established a team goal of simply making it through the exercise. In doing so, they stopped worrying about competing for time and concentrated their efforts on getting through the events in the most empowering way for all the team members. The strongest climbers went last so they could stand below the cargo net and spot the weaker climbers. The team members who'd been afraid now knew there would be some- one around to back them up.

The next day, Bart's team found itself in a surprising second- place position during the event, with the Australian team in first place—until they got to the cargo net. Empowered by their new unity, Bart's team made it across the net without incident.

The Australians, however, worked as individuals because each of them could easily climb the cargo net and did not see any need to support each other with spotters. One of them, now tired, made a mistake, fell from the top of the net, and broke his leg and collarbone. The paramedics came and took him away, disqualifying the Australian team. Astonishingly, Bart's team won the event.

During practice for the archery competition, Bart's team was as bad as they'd been in practices for the obstacle course. They rarely even hit the target. In practice sessions, while one person had his turn, the rest sat under a tree in the shade, paying no attention to the archer. During the real competition, however, energized by the obstacle course experience and the Talking Stick exercise the night before, they made a change of strategy. The entire team lined up behind each archer and concentrated all of its attention on the bull's-eye. The energy on the target was palpable and Bart's team went on to win the archery competition as well.

Now that the first two competitions were through, the teams finally learned about the "mystery event." It was a volleyball tournament. The members of Bart's team stared at each other, knowing they'd skipped the opportunity to practice for this event all week. This was especially problematic because some members of the team had never even touched a volleyball.

Taking the leadership role once again, Bart used the circumstances to bring the team together. At any given time, there would be five players on the court and five off. One player then rotated onto the court after every point so that everyone played. At every break in the play, Bart made sure that each member of the ten-member team passed the ball, even if they were not playing for that session. This focused the group and distracted the competition and in the end, Bart's inexperienced and underpracticed team came in second for this competition.

In the end, Bart's team put in the best overall results for the entire event of any team in ten years.

How did a group of "ninety-pound weaklings" perform at such an elevated level?

By becoming a Line of One.

Building a Breakthrough Culture Through the Line of One

Line of One is a building block for high-achieving organizations on a Breakthrough trajectory. It is the ability to create a solid and unified force of people and energy, all focused on accomplishing the same mission. In the previous story, every member of Bart's team had the same mission in mind—to get through the obstacle course. Because they worked in absolute unity, forgetting the disagreements and bad blood that surfaced during the week, they achieved even more. In business enterprises people work together day in and day out, but there generally isn't a final event to prepare for. Still, if there is a clear definition of team success that each member buys into, Breakthrough results follow.

Line of One is a value of the most powerful teams. It is a very old value, going back millennia. Ancient warriors used their own version of Line of One as their primary battle strategy. When they fought, they created a line in which each warrior used his shield to protect the warrior next to him. In turn, each warrior was protected by the shield of the warrior on his other side. This allowed each to wield his sword or spear in the most efficient way and created a barrier that was difficult to break. The Greeks called this kind of stand a phalanx; for the Saxons it was the Shield Wall. The bond of trust between the soldiers created a power that was indefatigable.

The Mongols had a system based on what they called *arbands,* units consisting of ten warriors who lived together with their families—eating together, fighting together, and looking out for each other with their families behind them, literally and figuratively. Through this, they created an army that was disciplined enough to conquer China. In fact, the Mongols were on the verge of conquering Europe and only turned back because of the death of the great Khan.

Line of One organizations work toward a common goal in a powerfully aligned and mutually supportive way. They do business differently and build a culture that thrives on bringing conflicts and disagreements out in the open for discussion, debate, and alignment (think of the word *alignment* as equivalent to A LINE MEANT to accomplish extraordinary results) prior to proceeding congruently with the action plan. This value is familiarly expressed in the phrase "One for all and all for one."

   Line of One companies are forces to be reckoned with. Like a phalanx of ancient warriors, the Line of One mind-set is nearly impossible to penetrate. Loyalty and unity prevail, and when one team member is flagging or stuck, the others pull him up. The lagging team member, because of the Line of One culture that exists within the business, accepts constructive feedback without perceiving it as criticism. The encouragement of the team becomes an energizing force, and the results are a renewed focus on the strategy and goals. Line of One creates a sense of pride among team members by recognizing the contribution of each individual in a group context.

   The concept of Line of One can be visually represented by a circle—a continuous, unbroken line. Inside the line, disagreements, conflicts, and differences are encouraged—building trust and increasing communication—until all parties reach a point of alignment. Alignment is communicated outside the circle as a symbol of unity. Decisions are executed with the knowledge that the entire team is behind the decision.

   Working in a Line of One is about uniting a team in purpose and values. It is not about uniformity; it is about individuals working in unity within common values. Imagine the power of a team that discusses issues openly until they reach a point of alignment instead of gossiping about issues behind the scenes. The openness creates a team that is fully supportive of the team decision regardless of what it is, and supportive of the subsequent actions of every member. The team is now a symbol of unity to the rest of the world. At the same time, every member can act with the confidence that he has the full trust and support of other team members—he can count on the team staying together in times of adversity.

   In the film *Spartacus,* the battle between the Romans and the slaves was bloody. After a great battle in which many were slain, Lawrence Olivier's Roman character, Crassus, announces, "Slaves you were and slaves you shall remain, but the terrible penalty of crucifixion has been set aside on the one condition that you identify the body or the living person of the slave called Spartacus."

One of the slaves, a character played by Kirk Douglas, steps forward.

"I am Spartacus!" he yells out.

Another slave steps forward. "I am Spartacus," he says.

Then another steps forward, and another, until every man joins in, calling out, "I am Spartacus!"

In this dramatic film moment, every individual was willing to put his life on the line for the rest. They were aligned—a Line of One. In business situations, this level of trust allows each member to take risks and perform to their fullest level of potential knowing that the team will be there next to them in times of adversity.

In most unsuccessful companies, individual interests prevail over the interests of the total company. Companies such as Enron have been destroyed by leaders and mangers who elected to work for personal benefits over the interests of the total team. In that kind of company, the disagreements and conflict occur in the background. The people there talk about the things that are not working instead of openly discussing problems and finding solutions. Rather than Gossiping Success, the employees gossip about the negative. Magical Thinking is suppressed because after any big meeting, one hears employees saying things like, "I wouldn't have made that decision," or, "What a ridiculous strategy." The questions and concerns that should have been brought to the forefront and resolved are brought out behind the scenes, and the negativity spreads, undermining the culture and the organization's opportunity for growth.

Instituting the Breakthrough principle of Line of One prevents this because such behavior is outside of the parameters of the culture. Leaders who instill Line of One thinking in their organizations create an environment where acting selfishly feels unnatural. The company operating in a Line of One is comprised of Full-On executives, leaders, and team members who aren't afraid to express themselves when they do not agree with something. On the surface, there may appear to be a great deal of conflict in a Line of One company, but this is healthy conflict, a free-flowing expression of ideas that is out in the open and addressed.

What We Can Learn from Geese

In the Breakthrough program, we introduce participants to the concept of Line of One via a story that captures the essence of Line of One thinking. As with so many of humanity's most inspiring stories, this one comes from nature. It is a story about how geese migrate together over thousands of miles twice every year. We present it this way:

As each goose flaps its wings, it creates uplift for the birds that follow.
Lesson: People who share a sense of community help each other get where they are going.
Flying in V-formation adds 70 percent extra flying range.
Lesson: If we have as much sense as geese, we will stay in formation and be ready to give and accept help.
When the lead goose tires, it drops into formation and another goose flies to point position.
Lesson: It pays to take turns doing the hard tasks. We should respect and protect each other's skills and resources.
Geese flying in formation honk to encourage those at the front.
Lesson: Our honking should be encouraging. This leads to individual empowerment and much greater production.
When a goose gets sick, two geese drop out of formation and follow it down to help and protect it.

Lesson: If we have as much sense as geese, we will stand by each other in difficult times as well as when we are strong.

This is a powerful and evocative illustration of Line of One and it never fails to connect with our clients when we present it.

Implementing the Line of One

When we go into companies with the Breakthrough program, our ultimate goal is to leave behind the tools, techniques, thought processes, and strategies to build a Line of One organization. We often tell the story of the world-class rugby team the New Zealand All Blacks. The All Blacks are a team rooted in deep tradition and they have a .740 winning percentage against teams from countries all across the globe. When the All Blacks attack, their strategy involves moving forward in a Line of One, with players ready to support each other. The player with the ball is not the only one moving forward—the entire team moves across the field. Some players are ready to receive the ball, while others run positions to cover the players on the other team, ready to defend. Other players run forward to deflect and confuse the opposition, but they all move as one toward the same goal, even though they each have independent functions. Most important, if one of the rugby players drops the ball, another player dives in immediately, picks up the ball, and runs.

Line of One organizations operate like the New Zealand All Blacks. When the ball is dropped in a Line of One organization— a marketing campaign is executed badly, sales projections fall below expectations, etc.—someone else picks up the ball and runs with it. This is possible because the culture consists of Magical Thinkers who utilize their Five Powers and work in congruence. Line of One companies focus on solutions, not on discussions about dropped balls or rumination about who is going to pick the ball up. In a Line of One organization, any individual at any time is ready, willing, and able to pick up the ball and run with it, no matter what function they belong to or who was responsible for dropping the ball in the first place.

The Line of One business culture is focused on the goals, outcomes, and future state of the company. Anything said or done is with the intention of empowering the team. A safe environment for expression is created with rituals like the Talking Stick (or whatever feels comfortable in that culture as a way of getting rid of background matter). The idea is to build a culture of acknowledgment and encouragement, not a culture of blaming and avoiding responsibility.

Creating the Line of One

In the Breakthrough program, we implement a Line of One symbolic exercise that helps people envision the concept. We ask everyone to form a circle facing inwards, toward the center of the room and to hold hands. Then, we ask them to close their eyes. This often generates a bit of uneasiness or discomfort. After all, one rarely, if ever, finds oneself in a posture like this with coworkers. The impact of this, however, is astounding. After a few moments, we say:

Here inside the line is where decisions are made, challenged, or changed. Here inside the line, people are free to express their opinions. Here inside the line, conflict is encouraged, acknowledged, and dealt with. Diversity of thought and opinion is welcomed.

After this, we ask participants to feel the strength and support of the circle. They are feeling the power of the Line of One. The exercise works because it sets in motion the future state, and the feeling that anything is possible within the Line of One.

Next, we ask everyone to turn around. We ask them to face outward, hold hands once again, and close their eyes. From this, participants receive a tangible representation of what the Line of One presents to the outside world—a unified body of people in alignment. Again, we speak the words we spoke earlier. When we finish, we ask the group if it is ready to face any challenge it encounters. The expressions on participants' faces often answer the question before we even ask.

When Phil Jackson coached the Chicago Bulls, he discovered that after a game, journalists would pull team members aside individually and ask leading questions about their feelings for other members of the team. Tired after an intense game, maybe frustrated over a tough loss or a bad individual performance, these players would say things about their teammates that they might regret later. The next day their comments would be displayed all over the news, creating problems in the locker room.

Jackson knew he would have to stop this. He had a big enough challenge trying to turn a group of some of hugely talented individuals (including Michael Jordan) into a truly awesome team. He created a back room as a sanctuary that only he, his players, and their coaches were allowed to enter. No one else could cross this space—not even team management and certainly not the media. After a game, the players would go directly from the game to the sanctuary where they could wind down and debrief together before going their separate ways. Each team member brought a personal object into the sanctuary that symbolized power for him. As a result, the sanctuary became the place where they would regenerate themselves as a team—as a Line of One.

Principles of the Line of One

A Line of One culture creates a high-performance environment that goes way beyond effective teamwork. We can see a number of key principles operating that both create and maintain this extraordinary environment:

- Trust
  - People feel safe when being candid—both about themselves (admitting their weaknesses, fears, or mistakes) and about the organization. Nothing is "un-discussable."
  - They know that team members will watch out for each other.
  - Everyone pulls their weight and does their share.
  - Everyone has the same agenda, overall goals, and intentions—and if not, they declare the differences.
  - Failures and mistakes are accepted as part of the learning process of the business.
  - People feel free to try new things and take risks without fear of punishment.

- Respect
  - Acknowledging and giving credit when it is due.
  - Giving public acknowledgement and praise for accomplishments.
  - Appreciating each other's strengths and skills.
  - Encouraging each other's unique contribution to and potential for the team.
  - Listening respectfully to the ideas and feelings of others without bias or prejudice creeping in.

❏ People may not particularly like each other but they do respect each other.

- Openness
  ❏ Open, honest, straightforward communication and actions.
  ❏ People feel free to say what's on their minds and what they feel.
  ❏ Dealing directly with conflict rather than avoiding it.
  ❏ Creating a nonjudgmental atmosphere.

- Accountability
  ❏ Commitment to the team's goal.
  ❏ Team members hold themselves individually accountable for the success of the entire team.
  ❏ The team feels collectively accountable for the success of every individual team member.
  ❏ Participating 100 percent.
  ❏ Asking, "What more can I contribute?"
  ❏ Making and keeping agreements with each other—doing what you say you will do.

- Alignment
  ❏ Creating an environment where people are open about their disagreements yet still have the ability to buy in even though they do not naturally agree.
  ❏ Coming to agreement on the general direction without requiring full agreement on every aspect of a strategy, goal, or plan.

- Empowerment
  ❏ Creating atmosphere of empowerment rather than victimhood.

❏ Ensuring everyone can exercise their Personal Powers.

❏ Involving all members with decision making.

❏ Allowing team members freedom to discover their own solutions.

❏ Facilitative (rather than directive) decision making and leadership.

❏ Clearing away the bureaucratic barriers to progress by the team—ensuring the team has the knowledge and skills necessary to make their own decisions and solve their own problems.

• Coaching and Feedback
  ❏ Team members mutually coach each other.
  ❏ Feedback is expected, requested, and skillfully given to improve performance.
  ❏ The team works to continuously improve its collective performance.

• Unity and Cooperation
  ❏ Understanding that unity is not uniformity.
  ❏ Fostering cooperation rather than competition between functions or business units.

An example of these principles comes via the story of Pierre Laubies. When Laubies joined the Campbell Soup Company as president of its European division, what he found was a collection of individual country companies ruled by their respective barons. There seemed to be more rivalry between these business units than there was against the actual competition.

Laubies knew that he needed to create a significant transformation and quickly. A Breakthrough program brought together the leadership teams of each of his five national companies (UK,

France, Germany, Italy, and Spain), his European leadership (based in Brussels), and the leadership teams for his key functions (supply chain, R&D, HR, sales and marketing). All told, about seventy people attended. We chose Portugal as the venue because it was a neutral country—Campbell did not have a business in this country. In addition, Portugal symbolized the edge of Europe, as from there one could look east across a continent of opportunity for a truly integrated European business. The Breakthrough program was designed to start with a four-day intensive, followed by a booster one month later, a booster three months after that, and then boosters every quarter for another year.

The first evening of the intensive, people joined together against the common enemy—Breakthrough. As usual, we needed to work our way through the inevitable resistance first-time participants had toward the program. On the second day, we had each team work on the background conversations it had for each of the other national country businesses. Here, we started to see what they really thought of each other—how the French saw the English, the Germans the Italians, etc. The background conversations and filters we saw here showed why these companies were not aligned and operating as one.

Each group was asked to share all of its background—unedited—with the other groups. We formed them into a large circle to do this. It quickly became an emotional experience as people unloaded issues and tensions that they'd carried for years.

The background exercise had a cathartic effect. We asked them to put all of this background on flipcharts and pile the pages into the center of the circle. We then asked them what they wanted to do with the pile. As one united group, they rushed into the center, tore up the papers, and stuffed the pieces into garbage bags. They declared that they would no longer live with this debilitating background between them. After this, we formed the Line of One, going through the same symbolic exercise we described earlier.

It was from this place, from the Line of One, that we now set out to create the New Future and the New European Business. At each stage, we reinforced the fact that we wanted disagreement. We wanted conflict. We wanted this out in the open so we could work with it or resolve it. The Leader, Pierre, was careful to use every opportunity to model these behaviors and principles.

We spent the rest of the intensive program living in the future we were creating, simulating it and testing how it would work. Participants left this first Breakthrough session with tremendous energy drawn from the ambitious aspiration to double the size of its business within three years to one billion Euros. The aspiration required Breakthrough thinking, behavior, and performance. It would not be achieved through Business as Usual. In fact, it could only be achieved by the leaders, the different organizations, and the people becoming a Line of One.

Other steps were required, of course, but by installing the Line of One culture first, we were able to accelerate the restructuring process and guarantee that it would be executed smoothly and effortlessly. We created the Billion Euro Team and over the next months, we enrolled more and more of the organizations into it. The team produced posters, which they put into every office and along the corridors. Their logo was a photo of a flying formation of snow geese.

Because of Pierre Laubies's Breakthrough leadership and the rapid evolution of the Line of One culture, Campbell Soup had a truly European business model within nine months of that first Breakthrough intensive. The European business grew to one billion Euros in just over two years.

Generative Learning

Organizations that utilize the Line of One put a premium on learning. If the goal is to keep the line as strong as possible and for every member of the team to be able to pick up the ball when necessary, the culture needs to strive for continuous learning and improvement. When an organization employs the concept of Generative Learning, it creates an environment where learning emerges from all aspects of the operation. Team members are encouraged to seek as much information as they can find and to share this information openly in conference rooms, corridors, and offices. The culture of the organization literally *foments* learning.

Breakthrough organizations never lose their desire to learn. Most important, no one in a Breakthrough organization feels that he is above learning. Even the CEO must be a sponge for new information. In fact, Breakthrough leaders understand and embrace their positions as role models for this Generative Learning environment by being as inquisitive and open to new ideas as possible.

The concept of Generative Learning underscores an organization's commitment to the development and growth of each individual. It is, after all, the individual and that individual's curiosity and quest for continuous improvement that makes the Line of One inviolate.

Why Don't All Teams Work as Line of One?

Imagine a work or home environment where conflict was encouraged and not dreaded. Imagine how the barriers would fall down if people were not afraid to talk about finances, tell their spouses about a big money blunder, or share something secretive that might lead to a major disagreement. Most people have trouble imagining such a thing. Instead, they avoid the disagreements, and communication becomes unclear and littered with the things in the background that people hold back. Line of One encourages open communication, but for most people, open communication is a scary endeavor—it involves a commitment to a higher level of risk, a willingness to eschew the comfort zone.

Most companies and teams within organizations don't work as a Line of One because they aren't equipped to do so or, if they are, they aren't willing to take real risks. In our current business environment, most companies fail to focus on a uniform strategy because it's just too hard, requires too much time and effort, or because the leader lacks the wisdom to implement one. In those cultures, the individuals reign. People in today's workplace do not want to be managed. They know they have a variety of options available to them, including entrepreneurship or working for the competition. Line of One leaders look for ways to get their people focused and engaged in what the business is doing.

In business enterprises, people tend to work together day in and day out without congruence because there is no common goal in sight. There is no match to win like the New Zealand All Blacks, no tangible reward or event to connect with aside from company revenue goals or team performance goals. The Line of One strategy is based on the assumption that there must be much more than that.

The Line of One business is Full-On and Congruent. The Line of One manager continually asks if he has a defined team goal with the mission of team success and if there is a sense of trust and a strong bond between team members.

The board of one company we worked with had to fire a newly hired CEO. He looked great on paper, but soon after he took the position, he began leaving a trail of disasters behind him. As it turned out, the CEO was driven by personal success. He'd made considerable personal accomplishments, but he was not at all concerned with the success of the companies that provided him with the means for his own achievements. He wasn't a Line of One leader.

Line of One leaders create organizations where the individual is celebrated but aligned with company goals. The goals of the company are just as important as the individual's success, and openness and transparency are encouraged. We said earlier that there was some measure of discomfort for those who do business in a Line of One. That's because life seems easier when one has nothing to risk, when one doesn't have to *truly* look at performance, examine the things that could be better, and listen to others. Rather than disagreeing, it seems easier simply to sit in a meeting, nod agreement to avoid conflict, and then express reservations to anyone outside that meeting or even those outside the company.

That approach might be safe (or at least *feel* safe), but it is not the path to Breakthrough.

The path to Breakthrough travels in a line—a Line of One.

Putting Line of One to Work

Obviously working as a Line of One makes any organization powerful and resilient. Still, developing a Line of One culture takes work and intentionality. It is unrealistic to think you can flip your organization to Line of One thinking overnight. Instead, take measured steps to get there. Put a team on a particular project and introduce them to the concept of Line of One.

Explain that you're not only looking for a particular outcome from the project, but that you are also looking for them to achieve this outcome with the specific Line of One concept in mind. Closely monitor how the team works together. Use the Feedback Frame to show them where they are succeeding in bringing a Line of One spirit to the project and where they are not.

Once you've started to utilize this approach on one project, start it on another with a different group of people. Give regular feedback to each group. Encourage Line of One thinking and show how the project team falters when it fails to act as a Line of One. Offer each team the resources necessary to make it easier to act as a Line of One and celebrate each implementation of the concept.

Utilize Gossip Success within your organization to get the message out about the accomplishments of each team. Underscore how Line of One made this success possible. You'll notice very quickly that others will seek to embrace this thinking. As this takes hold, introduce larger objectives for the entire organization. Explain that the company is ready to operate as a Line of One and utilize some of the tools in this chapter to make that a reality.

The entire team will be more powerful than you ever imagined.

CHAPTER NINE

THE BREAKTHROUGH LEADER

Smallpox is estimated to be responsible for three hundred to five hundred million deaths in the twentieth century. The disease originated more than three thousand years ago in Africa or China and became an epidemic in Europe during the Middle Ages. After contact with Europeans and Africans, a large part of the New World population died of smallpox. Smallpox was transmitted from person to person by air through tiny droplets of saliva or biofilm particles from sneezing. As cities grew, the disease grew rapidly along travel routes. As recently as 1967, the World Health Organization estimated that fifteen million people contracted the disease and that two million people died during that year from smallpox.

In 1966 when working as a medical missionary, Bill Foege was asked to check out reports of smallpox in a remote area of Nigeria. When he and his associates arrived in the village, they encountered a huge challenge. They found an outbreak raging and they did not have enough vaccine to inoculate everybody in the village. Nor were they likely to get enough vaccine to vaccinate the entire population in time to stop the spread of the deadly disease—something health authorities believed to be the only answer to stop smallpox.

Foege knew that he had to find a way to determine where the disease was spreading, identify those hot zones, and vaccinate quickly with the supply available. He studied the nature of the disease and consulted with members of his team to gather as much information as possible. Based on this work, he pioneered a plan that focused on the inner ring of the known infected individuals—finding those with the disease and mapping out the most likely routes of smallpox transmission based on their family relationships, daily activities, and transportation patterns. Foege's team used maps and radios to contact missionaries in the remote parts of Nigeria, asking them to send runners to every forest and village to identify smallpox cases. The runners set out on bare feet, found the villages where people had visible signs of the disease, and reported to Foege's team. Within twenty-four hours, Foege and his group pinpointed exactly where the hot zones were. They vaccinated the infected Nigerians as well as the inner ring of people most likely to encounter them.

The innovative vaccination strategy Foege developed for Nigeria was a resounding success. When Foege returned to Atlanta to report to the officials at the Centers for Disease Control, he proposed that they use this strategy to fight smallpox elsewhere, starting with India, Pakistan, and Bangladesh, countries where smallpox was spreading out of control. They targeted India first, but Indian health officials were reluctant to adopt this approach, believing that the only solution was mass vaccination—a problem, given the limited supply of vaccine.

In a CDC meeting to propose Foege's focused, inner-ring approach, there was considerable resistance until an Indian physician spoke up. "If one hut is on fire," the doctor said, "what sense does it make to pour water on all the houses in the village?" Partially swayed by the physician, the Indian government gave Foege a month to show he could contain the epidemic.

At this point, India reported one thousand smallpox cases each week, so Foege's plan had to be creative and extremely effective. Foege sent people house to house in this huge country to identify cases, with healthcare workers immediately following to vaccinate and contain the outbreaks. They worked as a Line of One, posting staff at shrines in local villages where people with smallpox went to pray to the deities. They talked with schoolchildren in remote villages and showed them pictures of smallpox, asking for their help in identifying anyone with the disease. In the major cities, where 1 percent of India's population was on the train, Foege's staff waited at the train station with the vaccination. In the remote villages, Foege was intentional about finding creative solutions. He met with a villager who had a talking drum, and the man beat on the drum in a rhythmic song until thousands gravitated into the village on foot. Foege's team vaccinated them all.

In one year, India went from the country with the highest rate of smallpox to a country with *zero* cases of smallpox.

In 1979, the World Health Organization declared the eradication of smallpox from Planet Earth, due partly to the Breakthrough thinking, persuasiveness, and persistence of Bill Foege. Because of his Breakthrough leadership in the smallpox campaign, Foege was named head of the CDC in 1977. Following his retirement from CDC, two presidents of the United States have asked Foege for his help. President Jimmy Carter invited Foege to become the executive director of the Carter Center and President Bill Clinton nominated Foege to be the next executive director of UNICEF. He subsequently became a senior medical adviser to the Bill and Melinda Gates Foundation.

The Lessons of the Breakthrough Leaders

Breakthrough leaders surround themselves with great people. They are self-aware, with an intentional focus on their own growth and development, while working to build the personal power of the people who work for them. Breakthrough leaders constantly inspire the organization to design the future and work toward it in a Line of One. Breakthrough leadership is about continually generating possibilities and leading others to be aware of their abilities to fulfill those possibilities. Breakthrough leadership is leading people and the organization from the Business as Usual trajectory to the Breakthrough trajectory.

The Breakthrough leaders we've worked with are intentional about their vision. Like Foege, they listen and observe, use what they learn to create a vision for the team, and then engage the team to bring that vision to life. Teams that operate this way can achieve extraordinary and sometimes unimaginable results.

How could a simple missionary rise to the ranks of one of the most prestigious leadership positions in the world? Foege began as the small man on the totem pole as a missionary when the CDC recruited him—a tiny voice in the war to eradicate disease. Chances are no one in management at the CDC even knew who Foege was then. They certainly know him now, though, because his leadership skills and insights propelled him upward. Foege is innovative, intentional, and unstoppable. He is an example of a Breakthrough leader.

One of the things that Breakthrough leaders understand is the value of modeling other great leaders. They observe the behaviors, character traits, and thought patterns of the leaders they admire and apply those skills to their own leadership approaches. They also know that it is possible to learn from anyone—not just people in leadership positions. There is something to learn from observing a waiter, a secretary, or a handyman—anyone who does his or her job well.

In our work implementing the Breakthrough program, we've observed a distinction between Business as Usual leaders (those who manage organizations and people) and Breakthrough leaders (those who *grow and build* people, growing themselves in the process). Business as Usual leaders tend to think from the past. They make comparisons to past success and often hold backgrounds and beliefs that keep them rooted in that past. An example of this type of Business as Usual mind-set is a leader who carries feelings, Limiting Beliefs, or backgrounds that might prevent him or her from doing business with a potential vendor, partner, or client solely because of those internal Limiting Beliefs. Destructive feelings like jealousy or cynicism drive their decisions. Whatever they believe about that other person may not be true at all, but the Business as Usual leader has built assumptions on that inner belief and it keeps him from his own growth.

The Business as Usual leader often makes fast and irreversible decisions guided by emotions. Individual preservation is important for many Business as Usual leaders. They may lead through intimidation or manipulation just to get things done, but this approach ultimately works against them and against the growth of the organization. We often find that a Business as Usual leader does not know what he does not know. There may be areas of incongruence in the way he thinks, feels, communicates, and acts, but he can't acknowledge these things, even when they are pointed out. His image of himself and his effectiveness is greater than the image others have of him.

The Business as Usual leader may have achieved a great amount of success, have a strong list of allies and supporters, and have a sparkling resume chronicling a long list of personal achievements. Eventually, however, the Business as Usual mindset limits how far such an individual can go because of his limiting, internal, Business as Usual philosophies.

On the other hand, Breakthrough leaders think from the future. They believe that anything is possible in the future, regardless of what has occurred in the past. Breakthrough leaders refuse to be tied to old business models built on past processes and strategies. The Breakthrough leader has a distinct focus on people versus processes, an intentional leadership style, and a high degree of self-awareness. This kind of leader builds a congruent culture that encourages individuals to blossom and unfold, respecting individual intrinsic motivators and desires. Breakthrough leaders recognize that every individual is motivated by something different and that motivations can change over time. They work to create an alignment toward organizational goals with people at the center of that focus. They are masters at using their personal power of insight, inspiration, and intentionality and continually draw from those skills to lead, manage, and coach the people within the organization. They are inspiring to themselves and others, and they keep the organization out of the comfort zone, firmly rooted on a Breakthrough trajectory to growth. The Breakthrough leader inspires and builds momentum.

We have observed five specific traits of Breakthrough leaders. These five distinctions separate the Breakthrough Leader from the Business as Usual leader. Breakthrough Leaders lead people by enrollment and engagement. They live the vision now. They raise standards. They act as leader, manager, and coach. And they create leaders. Sadly, Breakthrough Leadership is rare in twenty-first-century business. Bill Foege is a Breakthrough leader. So is Wayne Calloway, whose story we will tell in the next pages, as we explain the five distinctions of Breakthrough leaders. At the end of this chapter, we'll introduce you to a few more such leaders.

Distinction #1: Breakthrough Leaders Lead People by Enrollment and Engagement

Wayne Calloway grew up in Winston-Salem, North Carolina. His father worked as a laborer in a fabric plant near the town. Calloway went to Wake Forest University on a basketball scholarship and graduated with a degree in finance. After he finished college, Calloway joined the Pepsi-Cola Company, spending his next twenty-nine years there. He eventually moved up to become CEO of Frito-Lay and, after a very successful tenure, became CEO of PepsiCo in 1986.

During his time at PepsiCo, Wayne Calloway is credited with focusing the company's businesses and achieving some of the highest growth rates in the organization's history. Calloway's approach was that of a gentle, warm CEO who engaged and enrolled all PepsiCo people in shared values. He was known as a "hands-off" CEO, choosing decentralization instead of tighter controls and supervision, focusing on empowering people who were closest to the customers—"those who are on the front line."

This empowerment and continual transformation paid off. Growth rates of each business segment were historically high under Calloway's leadership. During the time he was CEO, PepsiCo generated a fourfold increase in revenues from eight billion to thirty-two billion dollars and grew market capitalization nearly sevenfold from seven billion to forty-six billion dollars.

Calloway believed that a focus on people-oriented culture was critical to the success of global corporations. In his mind—

and we agree—the nature of business conducted by global organizations requires a fundamentally different kind of leader, because people are different all over the globe. The best leaders will work through people rather than providing top-down, hard-nosed direction. Interpersonal skills are essential for a leader to enroll and engage people to perform at their fullest potential. Calloway believed that arrogance had no place in a good leader's portfolio of qualities.

Another key message of his was that strong leaders create an environment that enables groups of people to work together in productive and meaningful ways. He felt that congruence between a leader's objectives and the company's strategic objectives was essential for consistent growth of people and the business. When asked about his primary function at PepsiCo, he simply stated, "We take eagles and teach them to fly in formation."

Breakthrough leaders lead people, not companies. They recognize that leading, motivating, and coaching is about the people and not about an organization. Understanding what drives individual behavior is important, as is recognizing how to motivate and inspire. The Breakthrough leader observes others and knows that ultimately, people want to lead their own lives. Employees want to be empowered and inspired, but they want to travel their own journey.

A Breakthrough leader's power does not come from title or authority; it comes from authenticity and the ability to relate to people, enroll them in the journey, and engage their energies and emotions in the goals of the organization.

In the old paradigm, experience equaled knowledge and knowledge translated to leadership. That paradigm doesn't hold for the new generation of entrants into the business world. They see a global, connected, "flat" world. To them, experience means little because the rules of the game have changed. Breakthrough leaders can connect with this group because they never pigeonholed themselves into one paradigm. The Breakthrough leader works to inspire and empower the individual, and that means being flexible enough to relate at many different levels— even when the individual in question rebels against authority.

These leaders lead from the front with words and actions that are congruent. They recognize that you can't lead from the back and have a clear understanding of what's going on in the trenches. To be effective, the leader needs to be in front of the customer, and in front of and with the employees. The Breakthrough leader understands generational, cultural, and individual differences and intrinsic desires, because they lead people, not processes or organizations.

Distinction #2: Breakthrough Leaders Live the Vision Now

PepsiCo was founded in 1965 through the merger of the Pepsi-Cola Company and Frito-Lay. At this time, the company had sales of $510 million. In 1968, PepsiCo acquired North American Van Lines. They followed this with the acquisition of Wilson Sporting Goods in 1970, Pizza Hut in 1977, and Taco Bell in 1978. When Wayne Calloway became CEO of PepsiCo in 1986, the company was highly diversified in the food and non-food businesses. The company had expanded rapidly in different businesses and in many different countries. As a result, it was spread too thin and was losing ground in many areas to leaner competition.

Calloway knew that PepsiCo needed focus, and he knew that his company needed to live that new focus immediately. He created a new vision trained on food businesses, leadership development, decentralization of power, and employee engagement at every level and challenged every employee to begin thinking with the sense of this new vision right away. Within two years, Calloway sold off nonfood businesses such as Wilson Sporting Goods and North American Van Lines and refocused the company on food businesses. He also developed annual leadership talent review and succession planning processes and decentralized business decisions from corporate to individual divisions.

Breakthrough leaders know that "the vision" doesn't exist in some far-off future. The vision is where you come from each day. It is how you think, and how you act. Living the vision means making an intentional effort to achieve goals now and bring the future into the present.

Breakthrough Leaders live in alignment with their vision. They think the vision, act the vision, and communicate the vision. If a leader's goal were to create an environmentally friendly company, that leader would do everything possible to personify that vision immediately, even if it will take years to bring the vision to fruition completely. Office supplies, cleaning products, plants in the lobby, and even the food served in the company cafeteria would reflect the vision. The leader's personal choices, from his clothing to the car he drove, would symbolize his commitment to the vision. As soon as Wayne Calloway identified his new vision for PepsiCo, he personally lived the vision and inspired his entire organization to exemplify that vision, thereby speeding the company's progression into the future.

Living the vision now doesn't mean building Rome in a day. What it means is that every step a Breakthrough Leader takes is in some way in alignment with the vision. These little steps combine to create the future and evolve the entire organization in the process.

Distinction #3: Breakthrough Leaders Raise Standards

Calloway grew from a poor North Carolina boy to the position of CEO of one of the largest corporations in the United States. He accomplished this feat through hard work and by constantly raising standards of performance for himself and those who came in contact with him. In his own gentle way, he would urge PepsiCo executives to think independently while working together to stay ahead of the competition. "If everyone is thinking alike, then somebody is not thinking," he would often say.

He energized himself and his team by constantly reminding them of "the company in Atlanta" (Coca-Cola) and the need to stay focused. "Nothing focuses the mind better than the constant sight of a competitor who wants to wipe you off the map." He made it clear that the only way to prevent PepsiCo from being "wiped off the map" was to consistently strive for more than the company had accomplished in the past.

Breakthrough leaders set "impossibly high" standards for themselves. They understand that they need to demand more from themselves than they do from the people they lead. This goes beyond the simple notion of being a good role model. The Breakthrough leader believes that anything is possible; therefore, he consistently strives to achieve the *im*possible.

We tell the leaders of the organizations we work with that they have a responsibility to their people to raise their personal standards. A common mistake new leaders makes is to continue to operate at the level that got them their big promotion. That makes a certain amount of sense. After all, if they weren't already giving 110 percent, they never would have gotten the new job. Often, however, these leaders find that time passes and they fail to achieve all that they want to achieve. The reason is that they've unconsciously slipped into Business as Usual mode. They assume they're already "good enough," not realizing that the new promotion requires an entirely new level of standards.

When a leader raises his own standards, he raises the standards of the entire organization. By showing that there's never a point where one gets to rest on one's laurels, the Breakthrough leader sets the example that continual growth is an essential part of the company's culture.

Distinction #4: Breakthrough Leaders Are Leaders, Managers, and Coaches

Surinder joined Frito-Lay in 1982, when Wayne Calloway was president and CEO. During his entire one-hour interview with Wayne Calloway before he got the job, Calloway spoke for no more than ten minutes. He listened intently with eyes fixed on Surinder. At the end of the interview, he spoke in a warm gentle voice. "Surinder, we at Frito-Lay are simple people with a simple business. You have a good technical and business background and you seem like a nice fellow. As long as you are willing to work with the other folks at Frito-Lay to build the business, we would love to have you." The simple, folksy style of the president of a powerful company enrolled Surinder instantly.

Years later, Surinder had left PepsiCo to join Warner-Lambert as president of the Consumer Products R&D division. Two and a half years into his tenure at Warner-Lambert, Surinder got a call early one morning. It was Calloway on the phone. "Surinder," he said, "I would like you to come back to your family— the PepsiCo family. We need you here." So authentic was his request that Surinder left a higher-level position to return to PepsiCo.

A major reason for Surinder's move back to "his family" was

the level and quality of coaching he received from Wayne Calloway. Calloway's consistent messages in coaching were focused on leadership development, employee engagement, empowerment, raising the standards, shared values, and teamwork. Calloway once said, "I will bet most of the companies that are in life-or-death battles got into that kind of trouble because they did not give enough attention to developing their leaders."

Breakthrough leaders don't simply lead. They shift between three roles: leader, manager, and coach. They lead people, manage "stuff," and coach performance.

When leaders collapse those roles into one, they don't live up to their Breakthrough potential. The roles become jumbled with none of them done to their maximum level. For instance, we know an executive who puts every issue on his "to-do" list, operating as if he can manage every task. He clearly doesn't understand that managing is only one-third of his function.

It doesn't take people skills to manage paper and projects (stuff). However, it does take people skills to work with people. They are different jobs. When a leader acts as a manager, he should be working on timelines, projects, and deadlines—not developing staff. People cannot be managed. They manage themselves. A leader manages the tools, environment, and processes around people to help them succeed and empowers staff by giving them the tools and skills to manage themselves.

When a leader is working with his team and sees a performance issue, his role at that point is coaching. Again, this is a different function. It requires one-on-one attention, perhaps reinforcing a vision, providing help developing skills, or making sure the employee is in alignment with the overall goals of the company.

Great leaders understand the distinction between leader, manager, and coach and they sharpen their skills to become good at all three.

Distinction #5: Breakthrough Leaders Create Leaders

Wayne Calloway believed in knowing his people and developing great leaders. He believed that all executives needed to
know their key managers well enough to focus their development and opportunities in the right areas. At Frito-Lay, he personally reviewed the annual assessment and development plans
of the top one hundred executives. When he became the CEO
of PepsiCo, he extended these reviews to the top *six hundred*
executives.

In one of his famous and emotional speeches at PepsiCo's
annual meeting in Windsor, Canada, Calloway stressed the importance of people-focused culture. "Many people send me
leadership books to read," he said. "They think that advanced
leadership principles and processes are important for me to
know." Raising a pamphlet containing the names of all PepsiCo
executives, he continued, "I do not need to read all those books.
All I need for our business is this book."

It is a testament to Calloway's drive and ability to create
Breakthrough leaders that Roger Enrico came out of semi-
retirement to succeed Calloway as CEO when Calloway developed prostate cancer and retired in 1996 at the age of sixty.

The role of the Breakthrough leader is to create more leaders, not followers. Remember the core concept of Breakthrough:
to build the business, you must *build the people.* A company with one
powerful leader and a collection of acolytes is limited regardless of the leader's vision and talents. A Breakthrough company
needs people at every level who can lead in alignment with the
company's vision.

Creating leaders entails a certain amount of openness and
self-assurance from the Breakthrough leader. Someone who

feels threatened by the growth of the people who work for him is likely to stunt that growth (at least unconsciously). What the Breakthrough leader understands is that the organization's overall success is a reflection of his leadership. A staff that produces great results, growth, and innovation shows that the head of staff is a superb leader. A Breakthrough leader is never concerned about being "shown up" by the success of an employee. He knows that the employee's success is his success as well.

Let's look at a CEO as an example. A CEO's future success as a leader depends on the entire organization being able to generate and sustain transformational change. That means that creating high-quality leadership around them at all levels is critical to organizational growth. Breakthrough leaders aren't threatened or defensive about handing over control. They encourage growth.

If Wayne Calloway had not been such a Breakthrough leader, if he didn't understand that one of his key roles was to build leaders at every level, PepsiCo would have been in desperate straits when he fell ill. Instead, because he'd embraced his role so completely, another great leader was available to fill his shoes.

Meet Some More Breakthrough Leaders

Breakthrough leadership is all too rare in today's business world. There are, however, several exemplary leaders. The following three leaders embrace the five distinctions of a Breakthrough leader:

Rita Clifton, Chairman of Interbrand

Interbrand, an Omnicom company, is the world's leading brand consultancy and the pioneer of brand valuation. Rita Clifton, the UK company's chairman, works continually to build the people and the culture within her organization. Rita manages a massive international workforce and has a strong focus on her employees, but views her role in business as having an important, higher calling. "The world needs to change for the benefit of all people; and since business runs a great deal of our world, you need to change business," Rita has said. "We all have a mission to make the world a better place."

After graduating from Cambridge, Rita began her career in advertising, working at DMB&B and later at Saatchi & Saatchi. She's a member of the government's sustainable development commission and she lives her vision of a more enlightened business environment—including sustainable development and the creation of a healthier world on a daily basis. At Interbrand, she has created an atmosphere where her passion for people and her passion for improving the environment can thrive.

"Margaret Thatcher said in 1988 that the environment is something that business should be concerned about. Suddenly I was able to make that an area of focus within the business environment. You need to think about how you are living and its impact on future generations.

"There's a strong fear of failure a lot of leaders share but it doesn't have to be a destructive force. It can be a strong energy source. It gives you a future view. You have to be purposeful about planning out where you want to go."

Rita participated in several Breakthrough programs during which we utilized an exercise that we call Destination Technology. We encourage participants to write down the key things they want to accomplish in the future, to paint a picture of what they want as an ideal company and culture in the future, and then use this as a transformation tool to envision an outcome and then work backward from this goal to create the plan to achieve it. Wanting to lead a company that would help business be better and socially more responsible was high on Rita's list. As a Breakthrough Leader, Rita enrolls and engages her people in the vision she lives, and she works with a high level of intentionality to accomplish precisely that.

Bill Wrigley, Jr., CEO of Wrigley

Bill Wrigley, Jr., has a high level of self-awareness that gives him the ability to draw from his own experiences to affect change within the company. During some of the Breakthrough sessions we've implemented within Wrigley, there were times when the CEO jumped in and offered examples from his own life, which helped people open up, contribute, and see the ideas being presented. The only reason he was able to be the catalyst for such transformation within the company is that he can freely relate the experiences and struggles he's had in life, describing instances where he has grown and developed, and where he needs to develop more. He can do this because he is prepared to spend time looking inward. When the leader of a company has a high level of self-awareness, it extends outward to every individual and the culture as a whole. As a Breakthrough leader, he lives this vision, starting with himself.

At Wrigley, Bill Wrigley's self-awareness in the role he's played as a leader and in his own work life has led to the development of a new program for employees called Healthy Core. The program focuses on work/life balance, something that seems popular to talk about in corporate hallways but is rarely understood or implemented. Bill feels very strongly that people should not see more and more work and less and less life. He believes that talk about balancing work and life falls by the wayside when devices like BlackBerrys, Treos, Palm Pilots, and cell phones make work accessible twenty-four/seven. Bill Wrigley believes that work/life balance is a competency, not an entitlement. Either you're skillful at it, or you need to become skillful. The Wrigley Company can help by providing the tools and the skills training.

The Healthy Core program at Wrigley is a three-day immersion centered on the personal lives of employees, working on building self-awareness, and an understanding of who they are as individuals. He believes this program will help build and enhance the people in his organization and he knows that when you build and enhance people, you build and enhance the possibilities for the future of the company.

Kyle Zimmer, CEO of First Book

First Book is a Washington, D.C.–based nonprofit that has given away more than thirty-four million books to underprivileged kids. Kyle Zimmer founded the business with a single mission— to give children from low-income families the opportunity to read and own their first new books. By creating a business culture with employees who are altruistic and passionate about what they do, Zimmer has lived her vision and affected the lives of millions of underprivileged children. First Book has evolved into a global force, supported by business leaders, celebrities, and governments worldwide, growing from a small nonprofit into a premier literary organization. They recently entered into a partnership with the Japanese embassy to provide books to hurricane victims in the United States.

Zimmer's philosophy on leadership started with herself. She was working with a young child in a homeless shelter when she realized how little the kids had. Books were scarce and children had no way of learning about the world and the possibilities for their future. They had no hope, and it occurred to Zimmer that if she could give these children books, the words within could give them that hope. She raised her standards by acknowledging that it was possible to go from helping a handful of kids to a huge number if she put the right organization together. The results have been intensely rewarding.

"One night I was in the house working late and my six-year-old son asked me about my work," Zimmer said. "I told him that almost no one in the world gets to do what they love. But I am in love with what I do."

Zimmer had been a lawyer in private practice before she started First Book, and brought with her an intense enthusiasm about people and an understanding that people need to be passionate about what they do and have self-awareness about what they're passionate about before they can be truly successful.

"We want people who are very smart. We want people who look you in the eye and tell you they want to change the world. Those are the people who can fit into any position. When you create a culture like that—you truly can change the world."

Zimmer's leadership approach has helped to create a Breakthrough business culture for First Book.

"We hire people who have a passion for what they do. No matter what their background, if they come to us with a real desire to change the world, they're a great fit for this organization. And that's the hallmark of anyone who excels at anything. Whether you're a top athlete or a brilliant artist, if you approach what you do with your mind and heart and soul and hands you're likely to be unstoppable.

"I hire people who are collegial, and willing to thrive in a high-stress environment. It's high-stress not because of external factors or the typical corporate stressors like corporate reviews or competition, but we have high stress because we all realize and talk about daily, that there are children out there waiting for us. There are children who have nothing, who are waiting for their one book. If you hire people who see themselves as change makers, you can create change."

Zimmer actively creates leaders in her organization. She knows that there will always be more children to reach and that there's more than enough room within First Book for everyone to shine. By hiring people who love what they do and cultivating a culture that avoids defensiveness and internal strife, she has created a company where everyone is capable of adopting a leadership role.

Breakthrough leadership is a product of bold vision, intense focus, and hard work. There are very few "born leaders" in the world from a Breakthrough perspective, but it is a skill one can learn and nurture. In addition, Breakthrough leaders work continually to maintain these skills. As Bill Foege, Wayne Calloway, Rita Clifton, Bill Wrigley, Jr., and Kyle Zimmer know, Breakthrough leadership is about continuous effort. There are always new people to enroll and engage. There is always a new way to live the vision. Standards must continue to rise. Being a leader, manager, and coach requires constant refinement and flexibility. And every day provides an opportunity to create a new leader.

For the Breakthrough leader of a Breakthrough organization, it is never time for Business as Usual.

Putting Breakthrough Leadership to Work

Breakthrough leaders build great leaders. They focus on generational growth because they understand that the long-term growth of the organization comes from building successively better leaders with each generation. Your job as a leader is to make sure that the leaders of the next generation are even better than you are. No one else can do this. It must come from you. There's no room for insecurity. If you're worried that the success of your team will outshine your own, you're not cut out for the job.

To become a Breakthrough leader, you need to create a powerful, enrolling, and empowering vision for your organization— and create a clear picture of the role your leaders have in realizing that vision. Enroll your potential leaders. Engage their minds with convincing logic and their hearts by building an emotional attachment to the company's values. Again, no one else can do this. If you get your leaders on board, if they are emotionally attached, they will perform to their fullest potential and bring their teams along with them.

Perhaps nowhere else in Breakthrough is leading by example so important. You need to live the values of the company. You need to raise your own standards and live up to those standards. This allows you to raise the standards for your people. Remember at all times that you are a mentor. It is not your role to manage activities. It is your role to select, help, and coach your middle managers to become leaders. Remember the goal: generational growth. These middle managers are the future of the company and they will only be as good (and therefore your company will only be as good) as you lead them to be.

Your company should be filled with people with high levels of leadership potential. In sports, many great teams are built around the concept of "bench strength." The notion here is that if a starter is injured or needs a day off, someone on the bench can fill the role effectively. Your current leaders are your starters, but you should have potential leaders throughout the organization ready to assume bigger roles when those roles become available.

A Breakthrough leader is always thinking about tomorrow and building his people with the intention that tomorrow will be better than today.

CHAPTER TEN

ACHIEVING THE FUTURE

The way we look at the future affects what we do in the present. If a person believes that the future is unpredictable—maybe even questionable—she will primarily live for the present. Her actions will be oriented toward short term, and her plans will be shortsighted. Many businesses tend to operate this way, believing that the only thing they can control in any way is the here and now. These businesses when successful tend to be opportunistic, very effective at crisis management, since they operate from the assumption that the future is unknowable and that they therefore need to be ready for anything. Unfortunately, growth is difficult in this environment, because the company is set up for survival rather than thriving.

Others believe that the future is predictable, and the better one is able to predict the future, the more prepared one will be for it. This is a cause-and-effect mentality: if you get into the right school, you will get a better job; if you get a better job, you will have a better life, etc. This kind of thinking, which we call "linear timeline thinking," is based on the past. A person who thinks this way imagines that the future will largely resemble the past and is therefore knowable. Businesses that employ this kind of thinking breed a culture of "temperature takers." When some people get sick, they take their temperature constantly to see if they are getting better or worse, seeking to predict the future of their health by the present readings on the thermometer. In industry, when a company relies on past performance to predict the future, they create a future anchored in the past. When the future turns out to break in some way with the past, these businesses struggle. IBM is a good example of a company that was left in the past when it based its predictions of the future on an extrapolation of what had gone before and allowed Bill Gates to take its operating system for personal computers. At the time, IBM saw the future as hardware—big machines, not small personal computers. Bill Gates saw the future as the software, specifically operating systems. Gates created the future from his insight and not from the past. His insight eventually led to the Windows operating system used by more than 95 percent of computers today. IBM saw nothing in the past (or in their future) that would have predicted that Windows would become more important than the hardware they manufactured.

A third view of the future is that it is a fluid process. It is not fixed and it is not predictable based on the past. In this view, the future contains an infinite array of possibilities. People who think this way actually use their future vision to determine what they must do now in the present to propel them toward the future of their dreams. People who achieve what they want in life have compelling visions and goals that shape their actions now.

The Founding Fathers of the United States of America saw the future this way when they wrote the Declaration of Independence. They envisioned a new nation with a new form of government. They then created the path toward reaching the vision of a country where every man, woman, and child had the right to life, liberty, and the pursuit of happiness. The outstanding leaders who envisioned this new future knew that to attain it they would have to break with their past and chart a new course away from the old world of tyranny into a new world of democracy. They drew on their own "Breakthrough tools"—the empowering philosophies of the eighteenth-century Enlightenment—and used them to give birth to a new nation and a new way of life.

Businesses that adopt this vision of the future take their fates into their own hands—they take an active role in creating their future. Breakthrough thinkers believe that they can have any kind of future they want. They are intentional about this. They don't let others decide what their future will be. As Lance Armstrong once said, "The easiest way to predict the future is to create it."

Change is a choice. A person can create her future by mapping out her destination and creating change, or she can change when circumstances demand it and accept any outcome that comes her way. Breakthrough thinkers understand that the latter is not a useful option. They understand that change is the only path toward transformation. For them, change is a part of the Breakthrough journey, and they embrace it.

There are three types of change. The first is change by crisis. A crisis occurs in a person's life or business environment (a heart attack, an unwanted divorce, the loss of a job, etc.). The response is to do one's best simply to cope, because one naturally feels that there are few choices available. The cost of changing by crisis is usually very high, as it often involves the loss of dreams, ambitions, and a sense of security.

The second type of change is change by drift. A person notices that the world is changing and that other people are changing with it. She realizes that she needs to change with them and goes along with the flow of this change movement. Change by drift comes with some drawbacks. When one addresses change this way, one might not change quickly enough to stay competitive, and may find that the flow leads to a change that is less than ideal.

The third type of change is change by design. A person who changes by design might be successful already, but sees change as a chance to surpass the competition and create a new energy for growth in her life. Change by design embraces change as a choice. It involves identifying a destination and setting out with high intentionality to arrive there.

Destination Technology

A destination is a desired outcome, the place where one would like to be. In business and even in our personal lives, people spend much of their time drifting with no clear idea of where they want to go. They might have a vague idea that they want

Business as Usual Trajectory

something different in the future, but they don't have a precise destination in mind. For obvious reasons, if the destination is unclear, getting there is difficult.

If one were choosing to travel to a physical destination (let's say the Arc de Triomphe in Paris at 11 A.M., on July 26) one would use specific tools to accomplish that task. Analyses of various travel methods and the length of time each required. A budget. Maps. A schedule for arriving at the appropriate time on the given day. A calendar and a watch, of course. This is extremely basic as far as getting to the Arc de Triomphe is concerned, but when one thinks about destinations like improving one's relationship with one's spouse or children, or increasing the morale and motivation of employees, the precise details of the destination and the tools necessary to get there become much more complicated to define. Still, just as it is important to know exactly where one is going when traveling to the Arc de Triomphe, the more specific one is in defining one's life destinations, the easier it will be to get there.

The Breakthrough Destination Technology involves seven steps intended to help people design their futures.

Steps to Breakthrough Destination

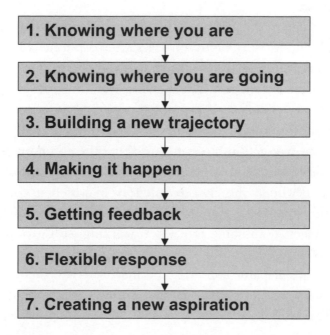

1. Knowing where you are
2. Knowing where you are going
3. Building a new trajectory
4. Making it happen
5. Getting feedback
6. Flexible response
7. Creating a new aspiration

Each step involves change and transformation. Together they chart a course towards the defined outcome, goal, or dream. A key distinction of Destination Technology is that after defining the destination, Destination Technology plans back from that future. Rather than having people move forward from their current reality with the intent of building a new future, Destination Technology guides people to *work backward* from their dreams. When people do this, the destination itself drives their actions, daily habits, thought processes, and communication congruently. This has two powerful benefits. First, it is easier to envision the future from the future—rather than from the now (which often, in fact, means creating the future from the past). Second, creating and planning the future from the desired future accelerates our progress toward that reality.

Step One: Know Where You Are

The first step in the process is for a person to understand where she is. When we work on this process with corporate participants in Breakthrough sessions, we ask them to create their current reality map. We suggest that they list everything and anything that has to do with their current state, being especially cognizant of the five "c"s: that consumers and customers are delighted with their products and services and that the company has the core competencies (people, capabilities, resources, tools, processes) to win in the chosen category in which it competes, keeping a watchful eye on the activities of the competition. This is an especially valuable tool when working with groups, as it leads to engagement and alignment among group members.

Once participants complete the map, we have them use the Feedback Frame to review the map to find out what is working, what is not working yet, what is missing, and what is possible. Based on this, they will generate a list of insights to define their current reality. They identify gaps, areas of incongruence, and places where the current reality might be dragging them down. From this foundation, they can then move on to envision the future.

Step Two: Know Where You Are Going

Once a person knows where she is, she can begin to identify where she is going. The key is to develop a well-defined outcome. To do this one must use Outcome Thinking. In our work with thousands of clients, it is amazing how few people naturally think about outcomes. Instead of thinking and saying what they really want, they focus on what they *don't* want. This type of thinking is Problem Thinking and it is based in the past. It represents a motivation to move away from a situation one does not want.

When we work with people who think this way, we let them go on for about ten minutes, then interrupt, and say, "So I've heard a lot of what you don't want. Now, what do you *really* want?" They visibly shift, their expression changes, their faces light up. We now have a different part of the brain working. They are now involved in Outcome Thinking and motivated toward what they want to have or want to be. Outcome Thinking and an Outcome Orientation is the way we start to shape the journey to that destination. It is how we motivate ourselves, our teams, and our organizations to move toward where we want to be.

Leaders often inadvertently focus on Problem Thinking. Bart recently attended a meeting where the president of a U.S. consumer goods company had called together his leaders because he felt the organization was not as focused as it could be. The group spent several hours defining and deciding what behaviors should stop. People gradually lost energy, became tired and defensive, and then argumentative. They were in Problem Thinking mode. I coached the president to shift the focus into deciding what the company wanted in the future. The energy and enthusiasm in the group changed dramatically. Now they were enthusiastic, creative, and far more intentional.

Organizations can be distinguished by whether their default mode is problem focused or outcome focused. The problem-focused organization will be mainly focused—and trying constantly to move away from—what they don't want. They tend not to be strategic. They tend to be more reactive and defensive. Outcome-focused organizations, on the other hand, are strategic. They have a clear vision of where they want to go.

In Breakthrough, we address this above the waterline (the conscious mind) and below the waterline (the unconscious mind). First, we engage the unconscious by guiding participants into a visualization where they time travel to spend a day in their futures. We ask them to imagine that they have achieved all they want to be—as individuals, as a team, as an organization. We ask them to imagine what their days will be like in the future, having achieved their vision—dealing with the organization, visiting with customers, working with their team, seeing results.

We then guide people into creating a map of the future. We ask small groups of participants to incorporate their individual futures together onto one map. They can draw, paint, and paste images or photographs to produce a multimedia, multisensory map that represents the reality and the emotional landscape of the future. People get inspired and excited as they construct this depiction of the future.

Then we engage the conscious mind, guiding participants to create well-defined outcomes for their futures and the futures of their organizations. The key at this stage is specificity. Deciding that one's goal is to be "the best," for example, is vague, and difficult to define. Everyone has a different definition for "the best" and it is that specific definition for that specific individual that needs to be identified here. We also tell people that it is important to define a goal that is within the control of themselves, their organizations, or their teams. The purpose of this is not to limit possibilities, but to identify things that are achievable. For example, if one's destination is to be chosen as one of the top ten Fortune 500 companies by *Fortune* magazine, the outcome is not entirely in one's power. When a destination involves factors completely out of one's control, it becomes harder to plot a course to that destination.

Once destinations are defined, we ask participants to identify the conditions that show that the destination has been reached. We call these "the conditions for success." We ask people to imagine having achieved what they really want. What does the destination look like? What do they see? What does it sound like? What does it feel like, physically and emotionally? What will be different from the way things are now? What will they have that they do not have now? What will they lack that they do have now? How will reaching a destination affect different aspects of their lives?

From here, we have them role-play the future. Seeing oneself in a new destination is a powerful tool for reaching that destination. If a person can see herself there, acting in this new role with new resources for a newly defined organization, she can truly understand the value of achieving this goal. This level of role-playing also helps to identify the key outcomes that will lead to the future. When a person sees herself in a new place, she can reflect on where she is now and identify what she needs to do to get where she wants to go. This allows her to "chunk" the future, devising a set of incremental outcomes—along with the conditions for satisfaction of each of those outcomes—that keeps her on the path to her destination.

Muhammad Ali used a version of this technique, which he

devised himself. A few days before a fight, he would go to the venue and stand in the ring. There, he would "go into a sort of trance." He would vividly imagine the fight being over and his being victorious. When he completed this visualization, he had his future history—all that was left to do was to live it. Ali told this story to a number of journalists over the years. Once, after he lost a fight, a journalist sarcastically asked how it was possible given Ali's "future history." Ali calmly told him, "I guess my opponent had mapped out a better future history for himself."

Step Three: Build a New Trajectory

Vision without action is hallucination. Imagining a powerful new destination is essential to growth, but it is meaningless if one doesn't set out on the journey to reach that destination. Designing a well-defined destination with specific details and clear conditions of success puts people on a different trajectory to reach their visions.

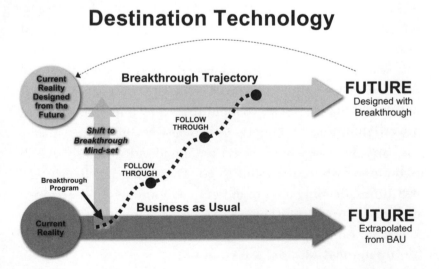

Every business and organization is on a trajectory. Most, however, are on a Business as Usual trajectory, doing the same things they've always done with limited goals and aspirations. When a business is on a Breakthrough trajectory, it has set a course for a new, ambitiously imagined destination. Having identified the destination in the previous step, one now needs to create a Breakthrough trajectory.

The Business as Usual trajectory is the default. It is created almost without thinking, certainly without intentionality by re-producing today who we were and what we did yesterday, and repeating this day by day. Before we've realized, we have built another three months of business as usual.

The Breakthrough trajectory by contrast builds each day from the intention of moving toward the desired future destina-tion for the business. This is a vastly different mind-set—a trans-formative mind-set that puts people and organizations on the pathway to the desired future. We do this by being different, by thinking differently, by acting differently.

The Breakthrough trajectory is built from the future. In Breakthrough sessions, we start from the established aspiration at five years out and the group details it as a series of specific, well-defined outcomes that together describe the aspirational enterprise of the future.

Next, we come back along the trajectory to three years out. We ask what needs to be in place three years from now—in terms of well-defined, measurable outcomes—to guarantee that we will deliver the aspiration in five years' time.

Next, we come back along the trajectory to one year out. What has to be in place in one year's time to guarantee that we get the outcomes we need in three years' time and guarantee that we deliver our aspiration in five years' time?

Next, we come back to one hundred days from now. What do we have to have started, accomplished, or in place to guarantee that we deliver our one-year outcomes, our three-year outcomes, and our five-year outcomes?

After this process, we have four sets of well-defined outcomes leading to the aspiration. These are the "what"s that we will deliver. Once we have built these anchor points or milestones, we now need to link the "how"s and the "who"s. From this, we have a Structure for Success.

At twenty-four, Bryan Meehan was one of the youngest brand managers in the group at a Breakthrough program for United Distillers (now part of Diageo). There, he learned from Bart the powerful distinction between building your future from the past versus the transformational mind-set of creating your future from the future. This changed Bryan forever. Years after that session, Bart walked into Fresh and Wild, one of the busiest organic supermarkets in Notting Hill in London. When he walked through the door, he encountered the owner—Bryan Meehan. During his Breakthrough session, Bryan had had a life-changing insight. He had visualized the future he wanted to achieve and realized that it was not going to be reached through his current career as marketer for a corporation.

Understanding that he was heading toward a future he didn't want, Bryan knew that he had to change the trajectory he was on, and he had to do it immediately. Bryan quit his job, left London, and went to Harvard Business School to complete his MBA. While at Harvard, Bryan studied an organic supermarket in Boston that had an incredibly successful business model. Bryan knew he could take this opportunity to London. He developed the business model, found investors, and opened the first Fresh and Wild in London. It became a runaway success and on the day Bart met him, he had ten supermarkets in high-income neighborhoods in London. Soon after, he sold the stores to the U.S. giant Whole Foods chain. A multimillionaire after ten years on his Breakthrough trajectory, he is now creating his next trajectory.

Step Four: Making It Happen

Once a person has mapped out a trajectory, she needs to put critical tools to work to make sure she arrives at her destination. Remember our trip to the Arc de Triomphe? The tools we needed there included maps, a watch, and timetables. The tools one needs to reach one's future destinations serve a similar purpose.

One tool is vision. It takes the powerful vision inside every individual to imagine a future destination. Once that destination is defined and a trajectory mapped out, however, vision still serves a vital role. The same vision that identified the future in the first place now serves to retain that image of the future in a person's mind as she heads off toward that destination. One key piece of advice we give participants in Breakthrough sessions is to "live your vision now." As we discussed earlier, this means adopting as much of that future lifestyle (office environment, clothing, methods of communication) as possible immediately. Doing so accelerates one's arrival at the envisioned future.

Another tool is focus. When one is driving, one doesn't reach a destination by making a turn at every road one encounters. Keeping one's "eye on the prize" is essential to reaching a destination. This means developing habits and honing skills specifically focused on the destination. Focus provides velocity.

Intentionality comes hand in hand with focus. Remember, this means not only having intentions, but also acting in a way that makes those intentions real. Intentionality gives a person power. When combined with focus (velocity), this power leads to acceleration and the faster attainment of a vision.

Perhaps the most important tool is the Line of One. It is very difficult to reach a destination if different members of a team are moving in different directions at the same time. Utilizing Line of One thinking and making sure that everyone is acting in a congruent fashion keeps a team on target for a destination.

John F. Kennedy's setting America on course to the moon is a powerful illustration of "making it happen." In the fifties, it was unimaginable that a human being would walk on the moon within two decades. Yet JFK showed inspired Breakthrough leadership to get us there. He set a big, ambitious aspiration—to put men on the moon and bring them back within the decade. This was impossible based on past performance, thinking, and behavior. Therefore, it could not be achieved using a Business as Usual approach.

JFK knew this was, "The most hazardous and dangerous and greatest adventure on which man has ever embarked," but he also knew how important it was to America's image of itself. He therefore declared this massive commitment publicly and took a stand for making it happen against significant opposition. He was Full-On and intentional about this goal. He used intentional language to describe his vision:

"We choose to go to the moon in this decade and do the other things, not because they are easy, but because they are hard, because that goal will serve to organize and measure the best of our energies and skills, because that challenge is one that we are willing to accept, one we are unwilling to postpone, and one which we intend to win, and the others, too."

Putting the first man on the moon was a great breakthrough in terms of science, technology, and engineering, but it was accomplished through the efforts of hundreds of thousands of people collaborating in ways that had never been done before; thinking and acting in ways that had never happened before.

JFK successfully enrolled different stakeholders into his vision. These stakeholders included Congress (who voted to approve the funding), the military (who wanted to spend the money on armaments), the astronauts (who would sit on top of thousands of gallons of liquid oxygen as it ignited to accelerate them toward their destination), the science and technology industries, taxpayers, and the rest of the free world.

When the vision he set in motion was accomplished, he had been dead for five years. Still, it was JFK who imagined the future and made it happen.

Step Five: Getting Feedback

When sailing, it is essential to tack and jibe, changing directions depending on the wind. However, it is sometimes difficult for the person in the boat to see how far off course she has drifted. Sometimes a person standing on the shoreline can see it better. The same holds true for anyone setting course on a new destination. Feedback is a key navigational tool.

Breakthrough leaders seek feedback constantly. They seek it from members of their organization for an inside perspective and they seek it from people outside of their organization for an outside perspective. One often knows intuitively if one is on course or not, but feedback offers a valuable additional perspective. Seeking feedback on a regular basis allows a person to make minor course corrections that keep her headed toward her destination. Without feedback, one could easily find oneself unknowingly headed toward the wrong place.

Business history is peppered with examples of great, successful companies that did not listen to the feedback coming from the real world and paid the price. The U.S. car industry in the seventies didn't listen to what that generation of drivers wanted from a car and lost those drivers to foreign car manufacturers. IBM closed its eyes and ears to the growing demand for personal computers until it was almost too late. In recent years, telecommunications corporations have only begun to awaken to the power and appeal of VOIP. Asking for and listening to feedback can be the difference between maintaining a competitive edge and becoming irrelevant in the market.

Step Six: Flexible Response

Getting good feedback is a valuable tool for staying on course. It is useless, however, if a person is unwilling to be flexible. Being flexible is very different from changing destinations. When one is flexible, one acknowledges that there are roadblocks and hurdles on the way to one's destination and that it is impossible to anticipate all of these before one sets out on one's journey. Flexible response means making the changes necessary to stay true to one's original destination.

When a person senses that something is preventing her from reaching her destination or she receives feedback from someone offering a similar observation, her job at that point is to adjust her trajectory. The new trajectory addresses the roadblock (the loss of a key team member, a change in the economic climate, an unexpected move by the competition, etc.) and makes the necessary course corrections while *always keeping the destination in mind.*

The story of Jeff Bezos and Amazon.com is the perfect example of flexibility at work. Bezos founded a company called Cadabra.com in 1994. Renaming it Amazon.com, Bezos started it as an online bookstore. The fundamental premise of the business was that an online company could offer millions of book titles for customers as compared to the several hundreds of thousands in brick-and-mortar stores and that readers wanted this breadth of selection. Over the next few years, Amazon grew at a steady pace. It is said that in the initial days, Amazon employees would roller-skate to fill orders from the warehouse to ensure on-time delivery. At the turn of the millennium, when the Internet bubble burst, many dot-com companies went bankrupt. Amazon was not immune. It survived, but only barely.

Soon Bezos realized that selling books online would not be sufficient. Amazon leveraged the speed and flexibility of its management, its business model, and its energetic employees to expand the business model from selling books to selling music CDs, videotapes, DVDs, software, consumer electronics, kitchen items, jewelry, sporting goods, beauty products, musical instruments, and many other household items. Soon, it started acquiring other companies that fit the Amazon business model and the company expanded internationally. The flexibility of Jeff Bezos has served Amazon extremely well. The revenues of the company have risen from zero in 1994 to more than seven billion dollars in 2005.

Step Seven: Creating a New Aspiration

Most people think about what is probable, not possible, and create a very small list of likely events predicted by and based on the past. The probable is based on a crystallized past, projected into the future. This is usually limited by filters (all based in the past), such as gender appropriate activities, finances, and health concerns.

What is possible is based on creating the future from the future, not from the past. It is taking into consideration all possible futures. This pulls us into our future instead of simply pushing us away from the past in the same direction. The Breakthrough world is not predicted or determined by past performances. In this world, a person creates the future she wants, jumps in, and starts living it. Likewise does an organization.

By the time a person reaches Step Seven, she is already well on her way toward achieving her future. At this point, it is time to apply Magical Thinking to imagine an even better, brighter future. Role-playing is valuable here. If one can imagine oneself at that achieved future, one can ask questions about a *new* future from that perspective. This allows for new aspirations and continual growth. By living in the future, we pull our future into the present.

With organizations, we are careful to ensure that as they near accomplishing their aspiration, they take time out of the business to create the new aspiration and the new time horizon. As they near the summit of the first mountain, the next mountain to be climbed appears above and behind it. If they don't do this, then they risk stagnation and decline rather than continual growth.

For an example of this, let's go back to the *Apollo* space program, this time looking at it from the perspective of the astronauts. This was the greatest journey undertaken by man and once accomplished, for some astronauts, it was difficult to find a challenge beyond that. With no new aspiration to take its place, some of the astronauts sank into a life of empty despair and, sadly, became casualties to depression or alcoholism.

One of our own clients, Pepsi-Cola, had a single-minded goal for years, to beat Coca-Cola in the U.S. market. They gradually caught up and then suddenly, in the early nineties, they accomplished their goal. After the jubilation and celebration, it occurred to many to think, "Now what?" They had no new aspiration to act upon. In the time it took to define one, the organization lost some of its best people because they no longer felt the hunger of the challenge. Pepsi's share started to slip, and before long, they were in second place again.

The Breakthrough change model involves first imagining one's current reality as a box. First, one changes things within the box (making sure one's current reality is congruent). Next, one breaks out of the box (creating a new destination). Then, one creates a *new* box (generating a new aspiration). This is a continual process, as people on a Breakthrough trajectory continually establish new boxes and break through those.

Chunking Time

The Breakthrough journey from where one is now to where one ultimately wants to be can seem overwhelming. It becomes less so when one utilizes mini-deadlines as a way to make larger deadlines and goals easier to manage. With this in mind, we teach people how to chunk work into doable tasks that can be accomplished in a given amount of time. We have studied this extensively and determined that twenty-minute chunks are optimum for most simple tasks. Less than this puts too much pressure on the task. More than this leads to unproductive processes such as mass-debating—where generating has stopped and been replaced by stating and restating opinions and positions. Chunking is especially valuable in meetings where the tendency is to become bogged down in details. Stopping after twenty minutes to evaluate progress and to check in on process has the magical effect of speeding things along.

Of course, some steps on the journey take much longer and cannot be rushed. It takes nine months to have a baby and rushing that process is, at the very least, dangerous. The same is true for some business developments. If one pushes unrealistic timescales, one puts unnecessary stress on an organization and runs the risk of preventing the organization from reaching its destination.

At the same time, however, setting sights too low is equally counterproductive. An organization should always attempt to reach its destination as quickly as realistically possible. This approach often leads to remarkable breakthroughs. During World War II, there was a need for a military headquarters in the United States. On Friday, August 8, 1941, General Leslie Richard Groves of the Department of Defense announced that he wanted the plans for the biggest office space in the world to be ready and on his desk on Monday. Most told him it couldn't be done. However, on Monday, August 11, plans landed on his desk. Construction began one month later. The Pentagon was operational within seven months, and the first occupants moved in on April 29, 1942. Construction of what has come to be known as the most efficient office space in the world was completed on January 15, 1943. General Groves understood his destination precisely and he arrived there with breakneck speed. Any organization with the same level of Intentionality can achieve as much.

Working in Power Time

There is another, more powerful way to achieve outcomes. Power Time is an incredibly powerful tool that generates considerable results in a very short period.

Even more than energy, time is the ultimate resource because, unlike energy or money, time cannot be regenerated. Even health can be recovered after an illness, but once time is spent, it is gone and cannot be regained.

Power Time shifts one's relationship with time. We can get a lot more done in a day just by shifting our relationship with time. We all can do this at times but we tend to do it unconsciously. Most of us can accomplish a huge amount on the day before taking a vacation—often without a great deal of extra effort or struggle. We just decide to be different and use time differently. Those who cannot or will not do this usually take a lot of their worklife with them on the vacation.

In the Breakthrough program, we have a twenty-minute exercise that guides people to see how they can use time differently and to get the distinction between Power Time and Ordinary Time. We ask participants in small teams of four or five people to draw a map that depicts the current reality of the organization we are coaching. These are the only directions we give, except to also say that that we are allotting twenty minutes to the exercise. At the end of the twenty minutes, we call a stop to the exercise. Invariably, participants ask us to allow more time, since no one has finished. We bring them back to their seats and illustrate how they have been working in Ordinary Time rather than Power Time. We then coach them in the Power Time Principles (listed below) and ask them to repeat the task, starting from scratch. The results of this second attempt are always dramatic with many teams completing the same task in half the time.

The Power Time Principles apply equally to twenty-minute Power Time meetings or projects with six-month deadlines. They are:

- Work within a Time Box. Allot a specific amount of time (say twenty minutes) and stick to it. Twenty minutes' Power Time can produce more quality outcomes than a lengthy meeting in which the participants engage in debating, distracting, and point scoring.

- Set a clear outcome to be accomplished within the time-frame. Ensure everyone is clear about the outcome.
- Always start on time.
- Start with yourself. Make sure you are Full-On, focused, and intentional on the required outcome. Work with full momentum, energy, and pace for the whole period.
- No debate, distraction, or drifting. When you find yourself mass-debating, start generating.
- Everyone participates. People who are not participating are not only a distraction but can also lower the energy and momentum of the whole group. If it's a meeting then only those who are actively involved need to be there.
- Always finish on time.

Power Time is not conventional time management. It is about changing one's state and one's beliefs as well as one's behavior around time management to get a Breakthrough result.

Power Time is an extremely valuable tool when used appropriately. As we stated earlier, one can't expect to have a baby or rebuild a company's infrastructure in twenty minutes. Still, we have found that one can usually easily accomplish as much in twenty minutes as one can in thirty.

Spread over days, months, and years, this speeds one into the future.

As we get to the end of this book, we want to bring you back around to the core message of Breakthrough:

To build a business, you must *build the people.*

Breakthrough companies achieve explosive growth—and futures beyond their wildest dreams—by developing their people to be the best they possibly can be. They encourage their people to think magically and heroically, setting out to do things that seem "impossible" and avoiding the kind of thinking that keeps great things from happening. They use the Five Powers of Insight, Inspiration, Intentionality, Intentional Language, and Congruence to establish bold visions and enroll others in those visions. They embrace Empowering Beliefs that keep the organization going even in tough times and set aside Limiting Beliefs that prevent the company from being its best. They employ Breakthrough Communications to move teams from ideas to actions and actions to results. They operate Full-On, inspiring their teams to use their energy in the most productive and effective ways. They work in a Line of One, creating a sense of alignment to the outside world while allowing open debate internally. They create clear aspirations, envisioning themselves as reaching those aspirations, and moving backward from there to achieve the future.

And they make sure to avoid buying a ticket for the Red Train of defensiveness and cynical thinking, staying on a cycle of creativity and possibility.

They know they can go anywhere when they are riding the Blue Train.

ACKNOWLEDGMENTS

We consider ourselves two of the most fortunate people. Over the past thirty-five years, individually and collectively, we have had the opportunity to work alongside some of the best leaders and organizations in the world.

First and foremost, our thanks go to one of the most inspiring leaders in business, Bill Wrigley, Jr. Bill personifies Breakthrough leadership. His focus, commitment, and contributions to the development of people at Wrigley are unparalleled in the industry. Through his discussions, valuable advice and counsel, and actions, he has enriched the principles, concepts, and tools of Breakthrough.

We are extremely grateful to the many leaders who contributed to this work through their experiences and insights. Particular thanks to Rita Clifton, Roger Enrico, Martin Grant, Pierre Laubies, Gary McCullough, Duke Petrovich, John Rudaizky, Martin Schlatter, Ralph Scozzafava, and Alan Weiss.

During this process of converting our ideas into a book, we have learned a lot about the literary world. Our journey into publishing has been guided by Peter Miller of PMA LitFilm, who became our literary agent and friend. Peter deserves our sincerest thanks for being a terrific guide through the winding path of the publishing world. Throughout our work on this book, Peter has been a pillar of resilience and persistence.

It was Peter who introduced us to one of the best writers and editors, Lou Aronica. Lou has done a marvelous job of communicating the spirit of Breakthrough in record time. We owe a ton of thanks to Lou for putting his heart and soul into helping us shape this book into an inspiring work.

Throughout the journey, we have enjoyed the terrific advice and counsel of Adrian Zackheim, our publisher at Portfolio. Adrian believed in this book from our first proposal and has enthusiastically encouraged us to deliver our vision.

Our thanks go to Adrienne Schultz and Will Weisser for their help and support in shepherding us through the editorial and publication process.

A special thanks to Tammy Kling, who worked closely with us on developing the original proposal and an early draft, and also for introducing us to our agent.

Our appreciation also goes to Donna Bernstein, Jennifer Dunne, Robin Gilman, and Kristi Saemann for their valuable contributions and dedication to the production of this book.

We owe a huge debt to Deborah von Hausen, who has been a creative force and co-creator of the Breakthrough Tools and the Breakthrough Program from the early days. She was instrumental in encouraging Bart to take his first steps as a Breakthrough leader. And to Max, who, now at age four, is already a wonderful coach for Bart in Magical Thinking.

As is true in our real life, our families get the last word of thanks and gratitude. We are indebted to Daven Kumar for his help in reviewing and revising the drafts, Janet Kumar for her unwavering support throughout her marriage to Surinder, and Surinder's family in India for their love and support throughout his life.

INDEX

Acceptance, and Blue Train, 96, 98
Accountability
    and Inpower, 60
    and Line of One, 164
Action
    and intentionality, 52–53
    New versus Business as Usual, 205–6
Activation energy, 142–43
Active listening. *See* Power listening
Akers, John, 147
Alignment, and Line of One, 164
Ali, Muhammad, 203–4
American Founding Fathers, 196–97
Appreciation, and Gossiping Success, 126
Armstrong, Lance, 197
Aspiration, new, creating, 211–13
Awareness, and Blue Train, 96

Background Conversations, 118–23
    and Background Filter, 118–20
    teaching team about, 129
Background Filters
    and Conversations, 118–20
    and perception, 73–76
    uncovering, importance of, 120–23
Beliefs
    Empowering Beliefs, 79–85
    and Iceberg model, 69–70
    Limiting Beliefs, 68–79

Berdusco, Roger, 50
Bezos, Jeff, 210–11
Blame story, 124
Blank, Arthur, 93–95, 97, 99, 101
Blue Train, 93–102
    basic concept, 11, 89
    behaviors related to, 96–100
    boarding, steps in, 98–100
    and creative cycle, 93–95
    and flow state, 95
    implementing, 101–2
Breakthrough
    basic principles, 4
    Blue Train, 93–102
    Business as Usual mind-set, 7–8
    Communication, 103–30
    Destination Technology, 9, 198–213
    development of, 16–18
    Empowering Beliefs, 79–85
    Full-Off organizations, 137–40
    Full-On organization, 141–49
    growth, conception of, 12–13
    Guess-So organizations, 140–41
    on ideal culture, 11, 18–19
    Leader, 176–93
    Limiting Beliefs in, 68–79
    Line of One, 155–71
    magical thinking, 8, 21–27, 36–41
    Personal Power, 45–64
    Power Time, 214–17
    Red Train in, 89–93

Breakthrough Communication,
103–30
  Background Conversations, 118–23
  Feedback Frame, 107–14
  Gossiping Success, 125–27
  implementing, 127–30, 128–30
  Intentional Language, 55–57
  negative effects, 123–25
  positive communicators, charac-
    teristics of, 127
  Powerful Conversations, 114–18
  Power Listening, 104–7
Breakthrough Leader, 176–93
  basic concept, 103
  versus Business as Usual leader,
    177–78
  characteristics of, 5–6, 176–87
  examples of, 5–6, 173–75, 178–92
  and Heroic Thinking, 29
  leadership, developing in others,
    57–60, 186–87, 192–93
  Wrigley as, 5–6, 9–11
Brin, Sergey, 36
Business as Usual
  leader, 177–78
  mind-set, 7–8
  versus New trajectory, 204–7

Calloway, Wayne, 178–87
Change
  resistance to, 10–11
  types of, 197–98
Chunking time, 213–14
Clifton, Rita, 187–89
Coaching, and Breakthrough Lead-
  ers, 184–85
Communication
  get-to-the-point versus detailed,
    106–7
  See also Breakthrough
    communication
Complaint story, 124
Confidence, and Empowering Be-
  liefs, 82–83
Congruence, 57–60
Conscious awareness
  Iceberg model, 69–70

versus unconscious. See Unconscious mind
Conversations, 114–18
  Background Conversations,
    118–23
  brands as, 117–18
  Feedback Conversation, 110–11
  foreground conversation, 119
  Gossiping Success, 125–27
  about outcome, 117–18
  and relationships, 114–15
  stories/metaphors, 115–16
Cooperation, and Line of One, 165
Creativity
  and Blue Train, 93–95, 97
  and magical thinking, 27
Crisis
  change by, 197
  and Full-Off, 137–40, 148
Cynical thinking, 24, 33–35
  negative effects of, 34–35

Defensiveness, Red Train, 90–93,
  98–99
Destination Technology, 198–213
  basic concept, 9
  Power Time, 214–17
  steps in, 199–213
DeVink, Lodewick, 80–81
Disappointment, and cynical think-
  ing, 34–35
Domino theory, 116
Drift, change by, 197–98

Edge exercise, 76–77
Edison, Thomas, 33, 48, 82–83, 84
Einstein, Albert, 82–83
Empower
  versus Inpower, 60
  and Line of One, 164–65
Empowering Beliefs, 79–85
  implementing, 83–85
Energy
  activation energy, 142–43
  Full-Off position, 137–40, 148
  Full-On position, 141–49
  function of, 136–38

Guess-So position, 138, 140–41, 144
high-negative, 146
high-positive, 146
and inspiration, 50
and intentional language, 55–56
low-negative, 146
low-positive, 145–46
Red Train versus Blue Train, 99–100
Enrico, Roger, 43–44, 46–59, 186

Failure
crisis and Full-Off, 137–40, 148
and resigned thinking, 31–32
and success, 84
Fear, and Limiting Beliefs, 78–79, 83
Feedback
and Destination Technology, 209–10
giving, lack of training in, 108
importance of, 107, 110–11, 209–10
and Line of One, 165
Feedback Frame, 107–14
components of, 109–10
and Destination Technology, 200–201
Feedback Conversation, 110–11
implementing, 128–29
and Personal Advisory Board, 35
Fight-or-flight, 91–92
Filters. See Background filters
Five powers
congruence, 57–60
Empower versus Inpower, 60
implementing, 61–64
Insight, 46–48
Inspiration, 49–51
Intentionality, 51–53
Intentional language, 53–57
Flexibility, and Destination Technology, 210–11
Flow state, and Blue Train, 95
Focus, and Destination Technology, 207
Foege, Bill, 173–75, 178

Full-Off, 137–40, 148
Full-On, 141–49
and activation energy, 142–43
leading organization into, 143–45, 147–49
Line of One businesses, 155–71
Future
Breakthrough Leader view of, 178
Destination Technology, 198–213
simulation of, 9
visualization of, 203–4

Gates, Bill, 196
Generate, and Blue Train, 97
Generative Learning, 168
Gerstner, Lou, 147
Goodes, Mel, 71, 80
Gossip, 123–27
Gossiping Success, 125–27, 129–30
negative, stopping, 125–27
negative communications related to, 124–25
Groves, Leslie Richard, 214
Growth
Breakthrough concept of, 12–13
and Full-On, 141–49
Guess-So, 138, 140–41, 144, 148

Heroic thinking, 27–29
of Breakthrough Leader, 29
and childhood/adolescence, 28
High-negative energy state, 146
High-positive energy state, 146

Iacocca, Lee, 147
Iceberg model, 69–70
Inner voice, as barrier to listening, 105–6
Innovation
and Full-On, 141–42
and insight, 48
and unconscious mind, 82–83
Inpower, versus Empower, 60
Insight, 46–48
types of, 47–48
Inspiration, 49–51

Intentionality, 51–53
Intentional language, 53–57

Jackson, Phil, 162
Jagger, Durk, 87
Johnson, Edward (Mead), 133
Journal, energy-monitoring, 148–49

Kennedy, John F., 208–9
Kumar, Surinder, 67–68, 70–71, 134, 184–85, 219–20

Land, Edwin, 21–22, 25, 27–30
Language, intentional, 53–57
Laubies, Pierre, 165–67
Leadership. *See* Breakthrough Leader
Learned helplessness story, 124–25
Learning, Generative Learning, 168
Letting go, and Blue Train, 96, 99
Limiting Beliefs, 8, 68–79
    and fear, 78–79, 83
    stripping away, 76–78, 83–84
Line of One, 155–71
    and Destination Technology, 208
    geese migration example, 159–60
    and Generative Learning, 168
    historical use of, 156
    implementing, 160–62, 165–67, 170–71
    organizations, features of, 156–57, 161
    principles of, 163–65
Listening. *See* Power listening
Lister, Joseph, 65
Low-negative energy state, 146
Low-positive energy state, 145–46

Magical thinking, 21–27, 36–41
    basic concept, 8
    and Blue Train, 94–95
    and children, 25–27
    example of, 21–22
Management, and Breakthrough Leaders, 184–85
Marcus, Bernard, 93–95, 97, 99, 101
Martyr story, 124

Meehan, Bryan, 206–7
Metaphors, as communication device, 115–16
Mind-sets
    Blue Train, 93–102
    Red Train, 89–93
Modeling, and Breakthrough Leaders, 176–77

Negative thinking
    cynical thinking, 24, 33–35
    and Limiting Beliefs, 70
    and Red Train, 90–91
    resigned thinking, 29–33
New Zealand All Blacks, 160

O'Neal, Jim, 49
Openness, and Line of One, 164
Optimism, and Blue Train, 89
Outcome Thinking, 201–2

Page, Larry, 36
Penney, James Cash, 143
Perception, and Background Filters, 73–76, 118–20
Perot, Ross, 131–32
Personal Advisory Board, role of, 35
Personal Power, meaning of, 45
Pessimism, and Red Train, 89
Pingle, Jack, 44
Positive thinking
    heroic thinking, 23, 27–29
    magical thinking, 21–27, 36–41
Pottash, Alan, 44
Power
    Personal Power, 45
    See also Five Powers
Power Listening, 104–7
    as active listening, 104, 106
    barriers to, 105–6
Power Time, 214–17
Priority projects, choosing right project, 62–63
Problem Thinking, 201–2

Red Train, 89–93
    basic concept, 10–11, 89
    switching to Blue Train, 98–100

Reinemund, Steve, 135–36, 141–42,
    144
Resigned thinking, 29–33
    negative effects of, 30–32
Respect, and Line of One, 163–64
Risk-taking
    and Blue Train, 96–97, 100
    and Full-On, 145
Russel, Paul, 57–58

Sayle, Bart, 2–3, 16–17, 77, 120–23,
    125–26, 151–55, 220
Skeptic, versus cynic, 34–35
Standard-setting, and Breakthrough
    Leaders, 183–84
Stories, as communication device,
    115–16

Talking Stick ritual, 153–54
Teamwork
    and congruence, 57–60
    and Line of One, 155–71
Thermoregulation, 136–37
Thinking
    cynical thinking, 24, 33–35
    fixed, negative effects, 24
    heroic thinking, 23, 27–29
    magical thinking, 21–27, 36–41
    Outcome Thinking, 201–2
    Problem Thinking, 201–2
    resigned thinking, 23, 29–33

Time
    chunking, 213–14
    Power Time, 214–17
Trajectory, New versus Usual trajec-
    tory, 204–7
Trust, and Line of One, 163
Tynan, Dr. Ronan, 82

Unconscious mind
    and beliefs, 68–69
    Destination Technology exercise,
        202–3
    and filters, 73–76
    and listening, 105
    positive resources of, 82–83
Unity, Line of One, 155–71

Value creation, and Gossiping
        Success, 126–27
Victim story, 124
Vision
    and Breakthrough Leaders, 181–82
    and Destination Technology, 207
Visualization, of future, 203–4

Walking the talk, 58–59
Wilson, Charles Erwin, 131
Wrigley, Bill, Jr., 2–6, 8–16, 189–90
Wrigley Company, transition of, 1–2

Zimmer, Kyle, 190–92

ABOUT THE AUTHORS

Dr. Surinder Kumar, Ph.D., a global leader in science and innovation, is the Chief Innovation Officer of the Wm. Wrigley Jr. Company in Chicago. Dr. Kumar has extensive innovation and business experience and, as far as we know, was the first chief innovation officer appointed in a U.S. corporation. Dr. Kumar is a member of the Executive Leadership Team at Wrigley and directs the team that creates innovative new products for worldwide markets. He has more than thirty years of experience in innovation and has served at some of the finest companies in the world, including Unilever, Quaker Oats, Mead Johnson, PepsiCo, Frito-Lay, and Warner-Lambert, where he served as president of Consumer Products R&D. During his tenure at various companies, his teams have launched hundreds of new products. He believes that innovation is an imperative for building enduring growth companies. The key to business growth through innovation, he believes, is highly energized people who work together toward a common goal as an aligned team. In *Riding the Blue Train,* he has incorporated his observations, knowledge, and practical experience into key insights for accelerating growth and building a culture that sustains innovation in corporations.

Dr. Kumar is an honored and distinguished member of *Who's Who* worldwide. He has been awarded seventeen patents, published many scientific papers, and served on several advisory boards. Organizational affiliations include board of trustees member, International Life Sciences Institute; member, advisory board of Penn State University; member, The Presidents Club, Ohio State University; and retired member, scientific advisory board, Rutgers University.

Dr. Kumar received the distinguished alumni award from Ohio State University, where he received his Ph.D. He has an MBA from the University of Chicago.

Dr. Bart Sayle, Ph.D., is a highly sought-after business adviser, speaker, and CEO coach. He is well known for his energizing and inspiring programs and speaking engagements where he shares his insights about culture, leadership, and innovation.

Bart Sayle has a kaleidoscopic background as a scientist, business leader, and entrepreneur with a lifelong interest in creativity, culture, and human nature. Driven by a vision that the world of business can be made much more effective, more creative, and more fulfilling for everyone, he has worked in the field of innovation and growth with business corporations for the past twenty-five years.

Bart Sayle is the creator of The Breakthrough Process®, now being used by Fortune 500 companies worldwide to design powerful futures for their organizations, their businesses, and their brands. More than twenty-five thousand business professionals have now participated in this process in more than thirty-five countries.

Bart Sayle has worked with some of the world's most successful companies, including Nike, Procter & Gamble, British Airways, Abbott Laboratories, The Wrigley Company, Visa, and Unilever.

Bart is currently working with CEOs and their executive teams to lead their organizations to achieve Breakthrough results—through an interactive, high-energy process that involves and engages clients strategically, creatively, and intellectually.

Dr. Bart Sayle is Chief Executive Officer of The Breakthrough Group, the worldwide leadership and innovation consultancy, based in London.

Learn more at www.GoBreakthrough.com

Dr. Kumar and Dr. Sayle are the founding partners of Innovation Doctors, now working with organizations to develop world-class innovation cultures. Visit their Web sites at www.innovationdoctors.com.

Readers can learn more about *Riding the Blue Train* and find additional materials to support this book at www.ridingthebluetrain.com.